2014

Jarek & Marie's

Thank you for first &
a part of my
Always

Adi

Own It

A Practical Guide to
Defying the Odds and
Claiming Your Life

ADI REDZIC

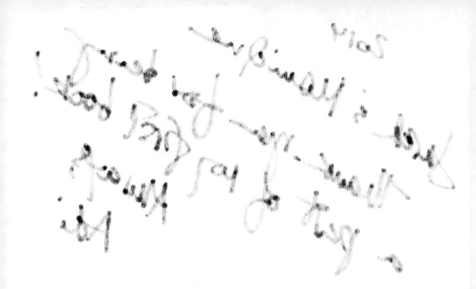

ISBN: 1502408554
ISBN-13: 978-1502408556

Author Headshot by Jared Chulski | Cover Design by Tami Jo Urban

To my parents,
Biljana and Sead Redzic

Thank you for having the courage to selflessly
let me go to pursue my own dreams.

To my grandma,
Magbulija (Buljka) Redzic
1927 – 2001

Thank you for the shining example of unconditional love
and for watching over me.

To all of you who have taught me about life
through your word and example.
You know who you are.

CONTENTS

FOREWORD

It was the Fall of 2002. I stood on the shores of the crystal-blue Adriatic Sea, throwing rocks into the water, my feet firmly planted on the sandy beach and my eyes focused on the horizon, the place where the Heavens meet the Earth. As wind caressed my neck and the seagulls kept me company, I wondered what my life would be like if I left Montenegro.

My homeland, once a part of the former Yugoslavia, had suffered tremendously in the preceding decade. At the end of the 20th century, the Balkans saw every tribe drawing its own border, deconstructing the artificially formed Yugoslavia. Everyone wanted their own page in the books of history, but to obtain these in the region -- dubbed a meeting place of East and West for thousands of years -- conflict was inevitable. Brother turned against brother and neighbor after neighbor. As Slovenia, Macedonia, Croatia, Bosnia and Herzegovina, Serbia, Montenegro, and Kosovo sought to weave a new thread of their complex ethnic identities within the auspices of three major faith traditions -- Orthodox-Christianity, Catholicism, and Islam; and as politicians rallied masses around ancient convictions, at least 250,000 people died, many of them civilian women and children, and more than three million became refugees. Women were raped, children massacred, and many were humiliated -- their remains displaced and never found.

1

As for the rest of us who were fortunate to survive and remain in our homes, the consequences continued to linger even as the conflicts subsided. Childhoods were spent in fear and poverty, our parents' dreams and hopes were destroyed, and economic instability, marked with hyper-inflation and astronomical unemployment rates, left most of us wanting. If you have seen images of people waiting in line for a loaf of bread, this was a reality in many parts of the former Yugoslavia.

While I did have a fervent desire to succeed, the audacity to hope, and a belief that, somehow, my future would be bright, I had no idea how I would get there. I did not even understand what that future would look like. My environment instead seemed to be offering something quite limited.

Yet, at least that day by the sea, I was a 15-year old teenager who dared to dream. The gates of my imagination were wide open, the fire of passion ignited, and I could not help but imagine a better life.

My ambition was fueled by involvement with UNICEF's Youth Parliaments, Local Democracy Agency, and several other organizations, which aimed to empower young people to stand up and work for democracy, peace, social justice, and mutual understanding in this troubled region. I did, like many of my peers, feel strengthened with this work. I did want to change the future landscape of my country. But, my ambitions were even greater. I wanted to experience, understand, and change the *world*. I wanted to *see* the world. I wanted to understand what life was like for people elsewhere. How did they deal with life's challenges?

Dreams of potential accomplishments ensued; the allure of a better life, of freedom, of happiness, and of love was intoxicating.

I had made my decision.

~

Henry Ford once said, "Whether you think you can or whether you think you can't, you are right."

I agree. When I first landed at the dimmed gates of Chicago's O'Hare airport in 2004, tightly gripping my two suitcases, with only $375 in my pockets, and a dream in my heart, I wondered: can I do it?

In the ten years since, I have encountered countless obstacles, yet have traveled a rewarding, albeit incredibly difficult, path.

Remembering the advice from a childhood friend, soon after my arrival to the United States, I wrote on three separate pieces of paper: "I want." "I can." and "I will succeed." And so I have.

I paid my way through private college and graduate school by winning scholarships and engaging in personal fundraising. I held six internships, ran a college newspaper, and taught a few classes. I helped revamp a center for spiritual development that hosted over a thousand programs annually and brought 11 faith traditions under the same roof. I led a coalition of 48 organizations, and more than 3,200 youth, in service to their communities. I helped establish a national think tank on financial security of young people, engaging thousands to think about their individual and our collective financial future. I have been humbled by invitations to offer motivational talks, serve on various national committees, lead workshops, and work with many brave individuals as they, too, chart their path to living their best life.

But back in 2004, I faced seemingly insurmountable challenges. As my host dad told me, years later, he didn't believe I was going to make it. And he -- and others -- had plenty of reasons to feel that way. I was a homesick foreigner in a new land where English was my second language. I was broke, melancholic, and lonely. I was also only 17 years old when I arrived.

Anyone who has been seventeen-year-old knows how difficult that age is.

As I navigated through my frequently tumultuous American journey, I never considered that what I was doing was something uncommon. If anything, I thought others were likely doing it much better. For example, I did not get a high score on my ACT test and I applied to colleges late in the process, missing many deadlines. I sometimes skipped classes and procrastinated. I had my share of failures, disappointments, betrayals, and struggles—both personal and professional. I felt lonely, lost and rejected, and often very confused. I felt inadequate. I took on jobs and projects that paid little in comparison to corporate opportunities I could have chased. And I missed many opportunities.

As time went on, however, and as I met new people, I discovered that while my determination to succeed was not unique, my methods were unconventional. I was -- and still am -- a "misfit" if you will; a square peg in a round hole.

The methods along my path may not work for everyone, but they have been rewarding for me. My intuition to take the road less traveled by, and trust the outcome, has made all the difference and has led me to meaningful success.

As my homage to a decade in the United States, the encouragement of many close friends and confidants, a checkpoint of all that I have learned, and, ultimately, a desire to positively affect others by sharing what I know, I have written this book. It is not a manifesto, nor is it a memoir. I do not believe that I have accomplished enough to write an autobiography, and I certainly do not claim to have answers to life's greatest challenges. Just like you, I am a work in progress.

However, I do believe that in observing, reading, working with others, and experiencing life in a passionate way -- both externally and internally -- I have accumulated lessons that I believe can make a difference to you. If nothing else, the lessons and examples in this little book are intended to offer a starting point in your own personal discovery – to encourage you to dream big and dare greatly in your own pursuit of fulfillment. I *know* that you want to succeed. I also know that you can.

Whether *you* think you can, or whether *you* think you can't, you are right.

HOW TO USE THIS BOOK

This book began as a quick guide for people to get into college, pay for it, and make the most out of it. As more people struggle to get an education and pay for it -- or even see value in it -- and as student loan debt continues to grow exponentially, I wanted to write something, in plain English, that might help others in their educational pursuits. I wanted them to know that if I was able to do it, against all odds, they could to. I wanted to write a direct, short guide that I wish I had when I was 17.

But then, as I began writing, I realized that there is no magic formula on how to get into college, pay for it, and make the most of it. Rather, it is all about the person that we are, our circumstances, our attitudes and beliefs about life, our approach, and how we live. So I began adding chapters that addressed topics that I believe are necessary for success *and* fulfillment in life. These chapters include lessons on persistence, on finding one's purpose, on defining values, on serving the world. Then, I asked a question about careers. If I am going to tell you to get a job, elsewhere in the book, shouldn't I also offer some tips on how to do that? Then, I felt I was doing disservice if I did not mention relationships, the central role they play in our lives, and how critical they are in our pursuit of happiness. Thus, there are now sections on both of these topics.

Furthermore, as the guy who runs iOme Challenge, a venture focused on the long-term financial security of young people, it made no sense that I would write a handbook of any kind without giving some practical money lessons and encouraging you to save for your retirement. There is an entire section on that, too, and I am grateful to my dear friend and financial wiz Allison Meeder for helping me put together some helpful information.

It all came together in the title "Own It" – because authentic happiness is not possible without taking responsibility for our own lives. It also took about five weeks to write it, design it, and publish it. The idea was to get the information out, so that it can help people, and worry about crafting better and more creative language later. Which is why the narrative is very direct, but sometimes also repetitive even after several revisions by independent editors. That said, I am more concerned about the lessons being useful, than about getting a critical nod for beautiful writing.

The book contains five sections: **on Life**, **on Relationships**, **on Learning**, **on Career**, and **on Money**. Each section has chapters that offer further guidance and lessons that have served me well and I am convinced will serve you well, too. You can peruse the book by going directly to a particular section, or you can read it as a whole. It is up to you. Some sections may resonate more than others.

After many revisions and much growth, this book is not only for high school or college students and their parents and teachers, but can be used by anyone else who wishes to find some answers to several of life's major topics. If you want tips on how to manage your money, read that section. If you want advice on relationships, check those chapters, and so on.

Since I am certain this book will grow and we will see updated editions, I welcome your input and ideas on how to improve it; what topics to include and which ones to expand upon. I would also love to hear which sections were most helpful to you in your quest to "Own It!".

PART ONE
How We Live

ADI REDZIC

1. RESPONSIBILITY IS KEY

The price of greatness is responsibility.
WINSTON CHURCHILL

We all have moments in life when a single conversation profoundly changes us. One such experience emerged from a conversation with a friend after she told me that "from the moment you wake up until the moment you go to sleep, you have a single most important responsibility: make yourself happy."

Although I fought this notion, suggesting that this would make me egotistical, her explanation and logic made sense. When we sit on an airplane, she continued, we are told that in the case of low-cabin pressure, we first place an oxygen mask on ourselves before we try to help others. How can we add to the happiness of other's in the world if we aren't happy or, at least, unless we are trying to be happy?

Being responsible for our own happiness does not mean we are permitted to infringe upon other people's happiness for the sake of our own. That's bullying. Responsibility means acting to change things, rather than simply complaining about them. Complaining and blaming is victimization -- putting the responsibility for our circumstances on others, including a greater power. Most of us have plenty of reasons to feel justified in blaming God, our parents, grandparents, siblings, former friends and lovers, and even the stranger in the next car for how we feel. That is about giving in and giving up.

"Giving in" is the belief that we cannot change our circumstances, that it will always be as it always has, that it's too late, that we aren't good enough or smart enough or pretty enough or strong enough. When we give in to these thoughts, we fall into an abyss of fear, which grows with time. We effectively relinquish the responsibility for our lives by putting everything in the hands of others. This is neither helpful nor fair, yet most of us do it.

Why we do it ... that's for another time. More important is the fact that giving in makes us afraid to pursue our dreams, speak up, be ourselves, live fully. We seek approval, we shrink in the face of criticism, and we fail in the single responsibility entrusted to us: to make ourselves happy.

I have partaken in this negativity many times. None of us is immune to it. For a long time, I lived a decidedly dual life of external appearances and internal narratives and struggles. Born at the outset of the Yugoslav wars that ravaged the region for the better part of my life there, I began questioning my own life and its meaning early on. Although I didn't understand everything around me, I observed it, and disliked a lot.

My childhood seemed short because I felt compelled to grow up quickly. I witnessed injustice, and was influenced by it. I saw suffering, bullying, and poverty. I was warned to mind my own business and get out of the way. I felt lonely, misunderstood and an outcast. I blamed others for my circumstances; feeling like the victim, I frequently envisioned myself pushed to the ground, unable to stand up.

Since then, however, I have learned that the difference between those of us who pursue greatness -- whatever that means to us -- and those who remain down is in the choices we make. Do we resolve to improve our situation, or do we give in to victimization?

I chose to take responsibility for my own happiness, and that has made all the difference.

Taking responsibility is not a one-time thing, however -- it is a daily occurrence. Each day, we are presented with situations and naysayers that test our resolve. Between growing up in war-torn Balkans, to crossing the ocean to find myself broke and lost, I had many opportunities to surrender to the habit of blame and victimization. Yet, I kept pushing ahead for three reasons: (1) If not me, then who? (2) If not now, then when? (3) Fighting even when the fighting gets tough is what winners do. Steel is hardened under fire, and so are we.

While I rarely felt like a winner early on, I badly wanted to be one, and I wasn't going to let the world get in the way. Especially not when I was 17 and had little to lose.

And -- it worked.

Everything written in this book is based on two premises:

1) You will take responsibility for your life and your pursuit of happiness. You can be upset, bitch, complain, and resist whatever you want, but at the end of the day: you own it. Things won't change unless you take action. This action can be minimal, but it's action nevertheless.

2) You will dream big and never give up. Persistence, in addition to responsibility, is a key ingredient for success.

ADI REDZIC

2. BE WHO YOU ARE

*Be who you are and say what you feel, because
those who mind don't matter, and those who
matter don't mind.*
DR. SEUSS

I have always enjoyed quotes. As a kid, I covered the
walls of my bedroom in the old country with quotes, and I
continued this practice in the United States. They inspired me
daily and reminded me of my aspirations. I wanted to matter.
These sayings reinforced my commitment and helped
motivate me. When it came to picking out quotes for my new
room in the United States, I stumbled upon the quote from
Dr. Seuss above. That one really resonated with me.

For a seventeen-year old immigrant, being "me" was
perhaps the hardest of all feats. Not because I did not want to
be myself, but because I wasn't sure what that "me" looked
like. Questions surrounding my heritage, relationships,
sexuality, dreams, values, body image, skills, and my future
were all fair-game questions, but answers were all but clear.
At that time, I didn't realize that "me" did not (nor should it)
have some specific definition, so I spent a lot of time
doubting myself: wondering what the right thing to say or do
was. I often felt guilty and anxious about situations; struggling
with a consistent feeling that I was doing things wrong. I had
plenty of reasons to feel this way: I barely had any friends

during the first few months of my senior year; my collegiate prospects were dim; I was broke, lonely, and nostalgic, with a sense of loss, for the people I had left behind.

Discovering "me" was a process that started a lot earlier, however. The war had a tremendous effect on all of us in the old country, defining our identities in more than one way. Beyond the effects of the war, I also wrestled with thousand-year-old traditions and societal norms that mandated I behave a certain way. But I was never wired to play a puppet to outdated traditions and unspoken rules. So, I questioned everything. I challenged authority even when I was told this was inappropriate. I wondered why I was criticized for my own dreams that were different from others, or why I should remain silent in the face of injustice out of fear of repercussions. Of course, I also wondered something even more fundamental: why would people who prayed to different gods want to kill each other?

These questions led me to studying human nature. They also pushed me into finding the best way to accept myself. While the journey continues, what I have discovered since is that the voice of others pales in comparison to our own. Being ourselves requires vulnerability, which opens us up to criticism. When we say what we feel, we risk being called wrong, which is why many of us follow the norms and rarely take risks.

But if we are not ourselves, who are we trying to be? Important to note is that being true to ourself is usually a small affair. It is not always about the big stuff -- it is how we live daily. Wearing what we like, or pursuing a cause or an interest that soothes our soul. For example, I love history but was ashamed of it for a while, because I didn't think it made me cool. I like painting, but it took me years before I shared it with people, because I was afraid they wouldn't think it was good. Yet, the bottom line is: who cares!

My struggles of being "me" have gone beyond the external into questioning the purpose of life and death, the existence of god, my own fundamental goodness, and the role each of us plays in this vast universe. We all have moments when we question our existence, blame the world for our circumstances, and wish -- even fantasize -- that our life was different in order to fit the norm. We do so because we struggle to accept that, at its core, life is not a fairytale with a particular beginning and ending, or that our lives are not easily molded from cookie-cutters; rather, we are each unique, fighting our own battles and doing the best we can.

Asking deep questions helps us find clarity and reach an understanding that each of us is meant to shine in our own way. However, it takes time to get there. It also takes courage to not blame the world, but accept that we are here, in this particular moment, with these specific challenges, for a reason.

It took me a while to understand that it was my experiences with loneliness and rejection, loss and violence, rules and criticisms, pessimism, scarcity, fatalism and many other obstacles that fueled my drive. It was *because* of them, not in spite of them, that I was driven to have the courage to dare. Out of adversity came the passion and resolve to succeed, no matter the obstacles. Much of this was subconscious, but all of it was rooted in my fervent and unwavering desire for freedom, happiness, and love. I wanted to be happy, but to get there, I needed to first break free from the shackles of my reality: my existing society, the scarcity, the dogma, and the personal beliefs and limitations.

It took me even longer to understand that releasing the shackles of our own reality is a process that begins when we summon the courage to let go of preconceived notions of who we are supposed to be and accept ourselves for who we actually are. The challenge is not to become someone; the real challenge is to be more of who we already are.

Sadly, most of us feel trapped in the stories we were told as children, the narratives imparted upon us by our environment, and our own beliefs, which are often rooted in self-depreciation, judgment, and harmful comparisons. These preclude us from taking a leap into self-discovery and self-acceptance. More to the point, we struggle to find a definition for ourselves. "If I am not this, then I must be that." This desire to define ourselves and others in a particular way, and give a label to our experience, is a reflection of our desire for stability and permanency. The truth is, the only constant thing in life is change.

"Being me" does not require a major production. It does not require that we define ourselves in any particular way or that we spend time figuring out how best to explain ourselves to others. Rather, being me means that we say and do what we feel and let the chips fall as they might.

All of my experiences influenced my journey. Some urged me to play a particular role, while others challenged me, in a real way, to dig deeper and remove the imposed masks, letting my true light shine. Somewhat prophetically, Seuss's quote urged me to remember that regardless of how blurry my vision of self was, I still needed to embrace it daily, the best I knew how, because over time and through practice, it would become clearer. As we get to know ourselves better and understand that no other person on Earth is like us, it becomes easier to let go of needing to fit in and of being affected by what others have to say.

As one of my former mentors said: show the world the middle finger and live out your own reality. This crude but truthful statement carries a powerful lesson that, although we have been taught otherwise, we don't need external validation to give ourselves the gift of self-love and acceptance. In fact, it is only when we accept ourselves and our reality that others can do the same.

In my personal experience, and through my coaching work, I have observed that discovering, accepting, and embracing who we are, along with trusting in our fundamental goodness, is one of the most difficult challenges. But, I can also attest that with greater acceptance comes greater peace, and although the process to get there requires time, commitment, hard work, and a lot of courage, it is worth it.

While I believe there is a critical difference between deciding to be who we are and living it out daily -- the latter being much harder -- there are several lessons that ring true in both instances:

1. Finding yourself takes time, and accepting your true self takes even longer. Take the time to do both and don't settle. That said, understand that the sooner you do it, the sooner will your life transform.

2. Commit to exploring who you are, what you like, what you dislike, and how you wish to live. Do so honestly and unequivocally. Pay attention to your gut feelings. Meditate, journal, find a therapist or a coach, and speak to trustworthy friends. Clarity will come.

3. Vulnerability is essential to our happiness. It is also essential in our relationships. If people can't accept you for who you are, how you feel, and what you think, do you really want them to accept you for who you are not? Vulnerability can be scary because some people will judge you, criticize you, doubt you, get upset, and push against you. Be vulnerable still, because those that are meant to truly be in your life, even when they dislike something or disagree, will be there.

4. It is much easier to be yourself than to try to be someone else. If you can't be an original, what makes you think you would be a good copy?

5. People can spot fakeness from a mile.

6. Your acceptance of yourself has nothing to do with others accepting you. For all intents and purposes, you may fully accept yourself, but the world may never accept you and you may not even feel the need to have them accept you. Your self-acceptance is what matters and where joy comes from; the rest is commentary.

7. Your job is to make yourself happy. The rest will sort itself out.

8. If people judge you, that's because they are uncomfortable. If people criticize you, that's because they feel inadequate in some way, but instead of changing themselves they are trying to change you. Take note: people may dislike and criticize your actions, and their views may be valid. But who you are and how you live your life is your business, and not somebody else's.

9. Be compassionate with yourself. Compassion is essential to acceptance, but you cannot have compassion for others unless you have compassion for yourself.

10. You are fundamentally good and so is everyone else. Don't *try* to be good; you already are. Instead, focus on accepting and living out your own goodness. We all make mistakes and do stupid things, but that does not diminish our fundamental goodness.

11. Do not compare yourself to others. This is a hard one in a world of materialism where we are constantly told that we are not good enough; that we should do or buy things that will make us better. Don't fall into the trap.

12. Authentic happiness is not possible unless we seek that happiness from within. Unless we take the time to find our true self, and then pursue those things in life -- friends, relationships, family, careers, hobbies, -- which truly resonate and matter to us, we will play someone else's storyline.

13. Don't play by other people's rules. A wise fisherman knows that there's more than one way to catch a fish.

14. Finally, we were all created for a particular reason. The point of our journey is to discover what that purpose is and to give it our all. There is no point in judging the cards that have been dealt to us. What we can do, however, is decide how we play it. Taking ownership of your life is powerful. It is cathartic. And it is done not by theorizing about life and trying to define it, but by living it.

Make it a quest to enjoy your life every day.

ADI REDZIC

3. FINDING YOUR PURPOSE

Your purpose in life is to find your purpose and give your life and soul to it.
THE BUDDHA

Not knowing our purpose in life is like taking a train ride without knowing why we are there. While the ride may be enjoyable at times, the lack of clarity -- of not knowing "why" we are there -- will inevitably cause confusion and discomfort. And fear. We cannot predict who will join us on the train, the detours we might face on the trip, or even when and where the train will stop. However, we can be deliberate in knowing our purpose and making the most of it.

For many of us, unfortunately, conversations about purpose aren't a part of a traditional upbringing or an educational system. Some faith-based schools, and church institutions, speak of service to others and service to a higher being -- and most of us harbor a desire to make a difference. Sometimes conversations involve discussing our individual vocation -- our calling in life -- which is a step in the right direction. However, it appears that for most of us, these discussions remain vague, leaving us with an idea of why we are here, not clarity of purpose. Without clarity, however, deliberate action is hard. It leaves us without specific tools on how to live out our purpose.

For example, a factory worker or an accountant may feel called to make a difference, but if they think their role is primarily to pay their bills, they are left with a void. In other words, our jobs are not our entire purpose. But if we don't know what our overall purpose is, it is hard to appreciate what we do on a daily basis, understand why we do it and how it makes a difference, change it if necessary, and discover how it relates to the bigger issue of why we are here.

Accordingly, discovering our purpose in life is our pressing responsibility. This world needs more people who come alive through their purpose. For many of us, happiness is not a matter of circumstance, but of choice. However, without the clarity of purpose, it is hard to make choices that bring contentment and happiness. As a result, too many people have jobs they hate and lives that offer less than they deserve. Our lives can, if we're not mindful, become a reflection of habits and a reaction to circumstances rather than a deliberate expression of our inner selves.

As with most things in life, discovering purpose is much easier than accepting it. When he was younger, one of my former mentors dreamed of becoming a lawyer and pursuing a life in politics. Somewhere along the way, something changed, and he discovered his true calling in higher education. Thankfully, he had enough insight to put his ego in check and follow his heart. This is the hard part of discovering and following our purpose: What if our purpose is not what those around us want us to pursue? What if it is not "cool enough" or lucrative? What if it is different than what we wanted as children?

My Dad is a mechanical engineer by training who spent his early life as a musician and much of his career as a business owner. So, when I told him I was going to study political science in college, he couldn't believe it. Why would I want to work in politics? He kindly, but sometimes too persistently, advised me to follow in the footsteps of my brother who is a software engineer or my sister who is in business. As recently as a year ago -- amid all my successes -- he asked when I would stop doing "that nonprofit work" in exchange for something more lucrative. I was able to chuckle, because I have accepted the importance of pursuing my own calling. (And my political science training is only a single reflection of my purpose -- a passion if you will -- rather than a purpose itself. It is a means to an end, not an end itself.)

Discovering our purpose, finding ways to express it, and then living it out is a *process*. Our purpose is bigger than our passions. Passions are many. I am passionate about music, painting, and traveling. I love watching movies. I am passionate about people, dogs, and plants. I am also passionate about politics, books, writing, teaching, and coaching. I can spend hours reading history, visiting museums, and taking in all the spiritual lessons I can grasp. I love psychology, and leading organizations by understanding business principles, strategy, and budgets. I also have to make a living, pay my bills, and fulfill other desires, such as making a difference and working with people. So which do I choose? If I chose a singular passion, my life would feel limited and I would get bored. On the other hand, if there is a bigger umbrella defining my existence, then these passions can be reflections of my purpose; they are the tools through which I manifest my own purpose. This affords me an opportunity to live a whole life, without limiting myself to a particular job, a particular hobby, or a particular passion. We all strive to be well-rounded beings, and life is short, so why spend time limiting ourselves?

For some of us, discovering and living out our purpose is straightforward. We know why we are here and we go for it. For most of us, however, the process is more complex. How do we find something that we love, among countless options, and love it enough to do it all day, every day, for the rest of our lives? People have said to me "find what you love and do that," and that's great advice, except ... how do I do that?

Finding Your Passions

What do you enjoy doing? Play a movie of your life and remember all those moments when you were really, truly, unequivocally happy and excited. Times when you were doing something you really enjoyed. Write them down. Make sure that you give yourself enough time to complete this exercise without distractions. Turn your phone and computer off. Really focus. Try to remember how you felt. You should feel a degree of excitement. Don't say you've never been happy. That's foolish. Don't worry about the content of these memories, their importance in your life, or their size (e.g. big events, small events, etc.). Just recall them and write them down. Once you are done, spend two to three minutes in silence and take a few deep breaths. Then, read out loud everything you wrote. Is there a pattern? Is there something that ties all of these experiences together? What were you doing at the time when they were happening? Are they all different experiences? Are they similar? Do some of them stick out more than others?

Those moments, those activities, those situations, and those events are the things that make you happy. They are your passions.

Let me illustrate.

When I was six years old, living in Montenegro, I wanted to start my first business: selling sodas to my peers at school. My best friend and neighbor at that time, Djoko, who was several years older than I, would purchase sodas wholesale directly from the factory and I would sell them to my classmates. The plan would have worked out beautifully had it not been for my parents who informed me that I had to pay taxes. That seemed too complicated, so I gave up. With my first entrepreneurial idea in the dumps, I ventured off to sell pretzel sticks dipped in Nutella hazelnut chocolate spread to my family and neighbors. This was somewhat lucrative, except for my older brother who kept taking them from the fridge without paying. Since I was powerless to change that (he had Mom's blessing), Djoko and I decided to start a "mail-in-order" business: we were going to draw posters of cartoon characters and sell them. Sadly, only so many people were interested in hand-drawn posters of He-Man and Ninja Turtles. This did not stop me for long, however. For some reason, I was drawn to the food industry -- in part because my Dad loved to eat, which meant he would pay for it -- so a few years later, in partnership with my younger cousin, Igor, and another friend, Mirko, we opened "Montenegro Cafe" within the confines of my home. The Cafe served a variety of sweets (e.g. ice cream and such) and we would sell them to my parents and their friends. The Cafe was successful but given the logistics and limited market, it closed soon after. This, however, marked one of the best summers of my childhood.

These memories are some of the best from my youth. They are also a solid expression of my entrepreneurial drive and passion. There were several other similar instances later on in my adolescence that reinforced this passion. For example, in Middle School, I found myself writing a single edition of "The School Moth," a news magazine I was hoping to launch. Although, an unimaginative principal rejected the project, it was because of this experience that I also discovered my love for writing, for journalism, and for expression.

Childhood is always a good place to look for our passions, because for kids, anything is possible, and so they freely pursue their passions. Sometimes, our opportunities are limited, but our imagination and passions still find a way to come through. Remember what those are. See if you can find them throughout your life and tie them together. Make sure you embrace the ones that still resonate with you. They will offer you joy and fulfillment. A collection of your passions will guide you to an answer about your purpose.

Another great way of finding your passions is through service to others. Often, even if we don't understand what's important to us or what makes us happy, when exposed to various causes and helping people and our community, we are able to find that spark and recognize what makes us tick and what we truly enjoy.

~

Discovering Your Purpose

It begins with a question: Why am I here?

Mary Oliver has a beautiful poem, "The Summer Day," which explains and expands this question beautifully: "Tell me, what is it you plan to do with your one wild and precious life?"

For a moment, imagine that I am sitting next to you asking that question. Can you answer it? If your answer is "I don't know," this is perhaps because you are too scared of facing it, or maybe because you have not given it enough thought. Imagine that the sky is the limit. Imagine that nothing in this world could stop you from achieving whatever it is you want. Don't think of it in terms of a job, or money, or other physical limitations. It is how you spend your time, your days ... your life. Consider that your basic needs are met, and with bluntness and utter honesty ask yourself: if there were no limits, material or otherwise, what would I enjoy doing every single day for the rest of my life?

Then, write it down.

First, write it in 32 words -- not individual words but full sentences.

Now, re-write it in 16 words. I am serious. Do it.

What about 8 words?

Write down the answer in 4 words; again, as a sentence.

What about 1 word?

What is your word?

Mine was "impact." At the time, I argued against this discovery because: a) I thought it was too generic; we all want to make impact; and, b) It sounded too idealistic. In fact, I felt that I would be limited by a desire to serve the world. My ego protested: what about *my* needs? So I tried the exercise again. No matter what I did or how many times I did it, I came up with two words: life and impact. Or: impacting life. Finally, at some point, I gave up on judging the viability of my purpose and decided to understand it instead. I wondered what it meant and why I came to that particular answer. What was it trying to tell me and what would I do with it? As I reflected on my life, my childhood and past experiences, my beliefs and values, the things that make me tick and those that make me upset, I understood that "impact" made sense. I understood that this is why I studied political science, for example, so that I could help find solutions to the socio-economic and political struggles of our age. This is why I work with nonprofits, why I coach and give motivational talks. This is also why I am writing this book.

Now, having a purpose goes beyond these examples. They are simply expressions of my purpose. Your purpose may be very different, and your expression of your own purpose will definitely be different than mine (this is where "being ourselves" comes in).

A wonderful thing about purpose is that it is with me daily; it is stable and no one can take it away. That is to say, when I wake up in the morning, I understand why I am here and I try to do something that day that will allow me to live out my purpose. If I don't succeed, there is always tomorrow. The next day, I am able to try again, and the journey continues. I no longer wonder what I am called to do. Now, I just wonder, how will I maximize my talents and do it to the best of my ability so that my impact has... well... the greatest impact possible.

~

Imagining the Achievement
Identifying our purpose is slightly easier than finding ways of living it out. But now that we have discovered it, we need to find best ways of living it out. This is where dreaming and passions meet reality and personal limitations. Grab a piece of paper and write down every possible way in which you would

love to live out your purpose. Dreams are essential in giving us motivation, allowing our desires and passions to fully express themselves, so don't hold back in writing them all down. However, make sure that they are authentic to you. Don't think of how others would do this -- only you. For example, while I recognize the critical difference physicians make in our lives, this is not something that resonates with me and it is not on my list. Similarly, while I love my niece and nephews and would do just about anything to protect them -- them and other children -- having kids of my own or even teaching them as a calling is simply not my cup of tea, at least not at this point in my life. I also love animals, but I could never see myself working at a zoo. And so on.

You have a list of things you would and wouldn't do, too; things that resonate and those that don't. It is essential that you are honest about those -- don't let preconceived notions or societal norms make you feel like you *should* love something when you don't. "Should" is a dangerous word. If you are struggling to come up with ideas, that is okay. Give yourself more time, try to dream for longer, think what you wanted to be when you were five years old, and let your imagination take you where you are meant to go. If that doesn't work, ask an objective and trustworthy friend to offer some insights. Get a coach or a therapist. Sometimes, we just need others who are thoughtful, creative, and sincere to trigger our imagination and pull us from the monotonous perceptions.

Once you have your list of ways in which you would love to live out your purpose, look at it for a while and see if you can find a pattern: all those things are likely your passions and things you engage in or think about regularly. Some of them also give you a fuzzy feeling in your stomach; that is to say, they make you more excited than others. Pay attention to them. Does any particular "way" stand out? Are you drawn more powerfully to one or the other? Once we have this list, we need to follow a process of elimination to get to the core and identify ways that resonate most with us, that match well with our talents, and are realistic.

For example, in an ideal world, my perfect way of impacting people would be by touching them deeply through music and singing ... I love music, I love singing, and I love being on stage. I also love the power of music and what it can do for people. That said, in the less than perfect world of ours, I am nearly tone deaf and you do not want to hear me sing. I *could* spend time and money to take voice lessons as a way of improving my skill. In fact, there was a professor at my alma mater who urged me to do just that. But this is where deliberate decision-making comes into play: yes, singing is a passion of mine, but just like the late Mother Theresa, I too only have 24 hours in a day. Why would I pursue a passion in which I could be mediocre at best, and touch only a handful of people, when I could otherwise focus on the passions that I am arguably more talented in -- like writing, or speaking, or building organizations, or coaching -- and make a greater impact?

For you or someone else, taking voice lessons may make sense, because your purpose is closely tied to that passion and you are likely more talented (don't even try to say that you don't have any talents; even making a good cup of coffee is talent, and not everyone can do it!). For someone else, getting a medical degree or driving a truck makes sense as the best way of living out his or her purpose.

To decide what is most important to us, and what aligns most closely with our purpose, we need to take a strategy from sporting competitions and create a bracket: list all of your "ways" in one bracket, and then use a process of elimination. That is to say, "way 1" will compete against "way 5" to move to the next round, and "way 3" and "way 12" will do the same, and so on. Follow this process until you are left with 4-6 ways. You may also have 1-2 ways and that is okay. Then ask yourself: Do these make me happy? Fulfilled? Can I see myself awake at five in the morning doing them? If the answer is "yes," then you need to pursue them. Money and everything else will follow. You are also likely to see only 3-4 of them stick. But those that stick are the ones you need to go after, regardless of where you are at today or what you thought about doing in the past.

The critical thing to understand about purpose and its manifestations is that it does not have to be lofty. We have all met people who, in the language of our arrogant mainstream perceptions, are doing seemingly unsatisfactory jobs (e.g. maids, assembly line and fast food workers, even homeless people, etc.) yet they seem the happiest people around. Do you know why that is? They let go of comparisons and feelings of inadequacy due to their "jobs" and focus on their purpose and on maximizing their overall happiness instead. They know that, at the end of the day, it is the content of our character and the expression of our inner purpose that matters. As I mentioned earlier, purpose is much, much larger than our day job. It is also by far more important.

~

Achieving Your Purpose
Now that we have identified our purpose and ways in which we can express it in order to maximize our talents and passions, we need to find a way to live it out. This is where daily and weekly tasks, and short-term and long-term goals, come into play. Every day, you can wake up with a few ideas about how you can live out your purpose. For example, if your purpose is to create, you can commit to create something new -- regardless of how small or large it is -- daily. Or weekly. If your purpose is to love, what about giving yourself some love daily? It is wrong to assume that our purpose has only to do with other people. Indeed, it is true that through others we are able reach our purpose and a full measure of happiness, but it would be foolish to exclude ourselves from the equation. How can we do much else for others if we can't, at some level, do the same for ourselves?

Equipped with the new knowledge of your purpose and ways to express it, spend some time thinking and writing down several Specific, Measurable, Achievable, Realistic, and Timely (SMART) goals that are in line with your purpose and act on them. You only need a few to get a taste of the power and happiness that come from the alignment of our greatest talents, our purpose, and our actions. As you complete the first few, repeat the process; add new ones down, expand them to include both short-term and long-term, and be on the lookout for additional opportunities for living your purpose through your passions.

Living purposefully requires mindfulness and intentness. It can get difficult at times, because it requires us to change our habits and, often, transform our thinking:: stand up, say "no" to unnecessary demands, and have the courage to dare. Playing to the beat of our own drum and pursuing our purpose comes with consequences, but it is better that we try and fail, and then do it all over again, than to never try.

It was legendary Mark Twain who said: "The two most important days in your life are the day you are born and the day you find out why."

4. DEFINING YOUR VALUES

Values aren't buses ... They're not
supposed to get us anywhere. They're
supposed to define who you are.
JENNIFER CRUSIE

If you pick up a book on values written by a philosopher, you might find yourself in the middle of a great debate on what "values" are. In my opinion, personal values are the building blocks of our character. They define who we are, how we treat others, and how we live our lives. They are guideposts -- our very own truth compass pointing in a direction that we need to follow.

I believe that all of us have values that we share, which represent *the* truth that is reflected in our fundamental goodness and that of others. This truth is how we know what is fundamentally right and what is fundamentally wrong, and it is only when we are unclear on this truth -- on these values -- that we do harm, cheat, lie, steal, and cause suffering to ourselves and others. If our compass points north, and our fundamental values are clear, we remain honest even when no one is watching. If we are clear on our values, they ground us and leave little room for misinterpretation and confusion, and they allow us to sleep well at night, knowing that our conscience is clear.

On the other hand, we also have a set of values that reflect our choices and define what we value in life. These values are what separate us from some people, who value different things than us, and bring us closer to others, who value the same ideals. To use the analogy from the last chapter: while our purpose answers why we are on the train, our values guide who we are and how we live, who we sit next to, and how we behave during the ride.

For example, I believe in justice wholeheartedly, and it is my value that I would jump into a fight if I saw "a big guy" bullying "a little guy." It is also my value that my word is sacred and that I should live honorably. Accordingly, I will do whatever I can to live up to it. I will speak truth. I will not cheat. And I will stand up to those who are not honorable, whenever I can and with whatever means I have. My value is to trust people until proven otherwise. It is my value to serve the world and make it a little better with whatever talents and abilities I have. My value is to adhere to the "platinum rule," and treat others how they want to be treated, and certainly no less than how I want to be treated. Accordingly, when faced with a choice, I will choose to do what is in alignment with my values. We are all capable of faltering in this area, but if we are very clear on our values, we can do our best to live them out and, most of the time, we will succeed.

When we have clarity about our values, they allow us to make decisions swiftly and with little agony, because we know what we value the most, and align us with the right people for us. They protect us from making stupid decisions in the face of pressure or criticism, or even worse, anger. And they remind us why we act, and need to act, in a certain way.

Sometimes, however, people struggle with their values. This happens for several reasons. First, they don't understand what values are, the differences between fundamental and personal values, or how to define them. Second, they are unclear on what their values are specifically, instead, they live according to the values of others, sometimes voluntarily and other times because those values are imposed on them. Third, life's events force our emotions to control our actions, disregarding our values. Finally, sometimes we give up on our values because the living gets tough, or because we witness others failing to live out their values so we decide we don't need to either.

Important notes:

1. Living out our own values has nothing to do with others; that is to say, we have *no* right to impose our personal values on others, and no one has the right to impose their personal values on us. We certainly have no power to control others, especially their hearts and minds. Values are a deeply personal thing. How we live is our prerogative; how others live is up to them and has nothing to do with us.

2. Some of our values will evolve as we experience life, learn and grow, and become more comfortable in our own skin. Some will stay the same. For example, it was only 150 and some years ago that slavery was alive and well in the United States. Similarly, interracial marriage was illegal fifty years ago, and our great-grandmothers did not have the right to vote a century ago. It is okay if our values change. The key thing is that we have to understand them, be honest about them, be humble as they change, and faithful about living them out.

Although our values may change throughout our lifetime, they are far more stable than our emotions. For example, on any given day, we may experience dozens of different emotions. In the morning, we may feel tired and groggy. As we drive to work, we may find ourselves getting angry at that guy that honked and cut us off, or feeling anxious about being late for work. As we get to work and get a message from our best friend, we may smile and feel happy. In the evening, we might see a movie that makes us laugh. Each time we feel something, we will be compelled to act differently. You are a lot more likely to snap at someone if you are feeling tired or irritated than if you are feeling happy and joyful. That said, it is because of our values that we don't hit a person in front of us because they cut us off in traffic or

35

why we don't take a baseball bat and hit our teacher for giving us a low grade. Values help us stay rational in the face of emotional distress while remaining faithful to our inner beliefs and views of the world.

With that said, consider this proposition:

VALUES → *EMOTIONS* → *ACTIONS*

That is to say, values guide our emotions and emotions guide our actions. If we are able to maintain this strategy, we will achieve a degree of balance in our lives that is necessary for happy living. This approach also allows us to live authentically, walking the talk by acting out of our values regardless of temporary emotions.

Most emotions are fleeting: they come and go depending on what is happening at any given moment. Our values, on the other hand, remain fairly constant. Values are ultimately our beliefs, which are based on long-standing emotions, experiences, and understanding of life. In other words, our values are a collection of emotions, experiences, and comprehension, and they exist to guide our life over the long haul, not in a single moment. Of course, there are situations in life when emotions will take over, regardless. But keeping this formula in mind, and deliberately embracing it, allows us to know what the right decision is even as our mind is blurry. No matter what is going on, if we have clarity in our values, we can ask: *What is the right thing to do? What do I believe is an appropriate response? What will I regret (or not regret) tomorrow or ten years from now?*

These questions are also the ones we ask when we begin to define our values. *What is important to me? What do I care about? What do I stand for?* This last question is especially potent because it hits on the main premise behind values: what is your character?

As I mentioned before, there are fundamental values such as "don't kill," or "don't steal," and then there are more nuanced ones such as "don't react if angry," or "count to ten before saying anything." Compassion, empathy, kindness, understanding, approachability, courage, creativity, assertiveness, consistency, reliability, truthfulness, and hospitality are all examples of values. But values also can be to not eat meat, to pray a certain way, to dress in a particular fashion, to not use drugs or binge on food or alcohol, and so on. Naturally, the more fundamental values will take precedence over the nuanced ones. In either case, our decision to act on our values -- and which values specifically - is a matter of choice and we make that choice by consciously, deliberately, and clearly defining our values and committing to them. We are not always able to live up to these values. However, each time we do, it becomes easier the next time, and we strengthen our character and feel a sense of fulfillment.

For example, when I was running the newspaper in college, and we reported on some touchy subjects, it was my values of truth and justice that guided my decision-making. Believe me, I was scared and at times confused on what the right course of action was. However, once I asked myself about my values, the answer that came was clear: pursue the truth no matter where it leads. From then on, my course of action was deliberate. Knowing what our values are, and calling upon them when making decisions, is important because it gives us clarity. My experience with the newspaper strengthened my character, my clarity of conviction, and gave me the courage the next time I was in a similar situation (and I have been many times since). Ultimately, clarity of our values gives us the motivation and the courage to live them out. When we have no values, when we don't stand for something in particular, we are likely to fall for anything. And this is often a definition of people with weak characters.

With that said, *how will you live your life? Where does your compass point to? What is important to you? What do you stand for? What would you die for? What is right? What is wrong?*

Remember, there's a difference between what is right and what is legal. Laws, traditions, and practices can change on a whim, and they often do. There are many people who observe traditions and practices, and who have never broken any laws, but they lack common decency and respect. Therefore, when discovering your own values, don't worry about the truth of others, but only of your own truth. Make sure you know what is right and what is wrong -- and honor that, as honestly as you can.

Additionally, be mindful of "brainwashing" you may have experienced throughout your life -- make sure that the values you write down are your own. For example, my Dad does not like standing out. He believes that it is better to live a quiet life, in peace and contentment. On the other hand, I am a firm believer that we find contentment by living large, standing up and working for what we believe in, even if that means we ruffle feathers along the way. In fact, I believe that we *should* ruffle feathers, and shake up the status quo, if that means we will bring more goodness and more justice to this world. I do not believe we should sit down and shy away from issues that are important to us.

Also, his definition of happiness and the way life should be lived is in many ways boring to me. This is nothing against my Dad, of course; it is simply a testament to how different father and son can be. I respect his way of life -- and his understanding of life -- and I love my Dad, but that doesn't mean I should adhere to the same values. Neither his nor my values are better than the other; they are just different. We can still respect and love each other, even when we disagree. I mention this story to highlight how important it is that you define your own values regardless of the values of your family or friends. Because, it is only when your values are your own that you will trust them and live them out fully and authentically.

It takes time to discover your own values, make sure they are your own, clarify them by writing them down, and cement them through action and practice. They will not come to you unless you think about them -- unless you feel within you the answers to the "what is important to you?" question, and engineer a set of values that works for you. You may be unclear on some, especially because you may lack certain experiences, but that doesn't mean you cannot make a choice that seems right to you. Your values can and will change as you go through life, but having values that may change is far better than not having any values.

So, when we talk about taking the time to find yourself, discovering your values falls under that time. Knowing your fundamental values and what you value in life is important, because it defines how you live. It also helps you build relationships with people whose values align with your own. Your values allow you to live out your purpose more fully. They help people understand who you are, what you stand for, and ultimately what they can expect from you. Some people will like you, others won't, but by knowing your own values you will be true to yourself.

Just like you did when you discovered your purpose, give yourself time to outline, in specific terms, what your values are. See if you can recall experiences from your life that have shaped your values and in which direction. Consider those values that have been imparted upon you by family or society, and which you dislike and would like to let go, and also those that you would like to keep. One way of doing this is by writing down experiences that brought you joy and a sense of accomplishment, and also those that brought you pain and hurt. See if you can group these experiences, both positive and negative, into two separate piles and identify common threads in each of them. *What have you learned from those experiences? How would you do things differently now that you have the power of hindsight? What would you advise your younger-self?* Write these down and be as succinct as possible. As you consider what you have written, are there particular words that describe how you ought to operate in the future? If so, those words are likely the descriptors of your values (e.g. courage, thoughtfulness, carefulness, eagerness, etc.)

You can also group your values into the core or fundamental ones, and the nuanced or personal ones. That might help you find greater clarity. Talk to a coach, therapist, or a friend that you respect because of what they stand for. Consider speaking with those who will encourage your own authentic voice and won't push on you their views of the world.

Imagine yourself in different scenarios and see how you would react. *What kind of person do you want to be?* In all of these exercises, pay close attention to your body and your intuition for they will not lead you astray. You may even ask yourself questions such as, "could I live with this outcome?" or "would I ever forgive myself if I ... (fill in the blank?)" These deep and somewhat fatalistic questions can offer insights about what you would and wouldn't do. Of course, none of us knows what will really happen until it actually happens -- iron is forged by fire -- that is to say: our character is forged through experience. But it is much better and easier to forge a character when we know what we want that character to be like; when we know the kind of person we are and want to be.

Which brings me to my final point: when you outline what you value, go test it out. We use our value-based judgments daily, we make choices that are guided by our values even if we don't realize it, and we act from imbedded values even if we don't call them that. So, when you clarify what your values are, look for opportunities every day to live them out. Test them out. Make them stronger. By being mindful about them, your values will align with your actions and they will forge your character through practice.

In conclusion, I will leave you with a thought attributed to Mahatma Gandhi:

> *Your beliefs become your thoughts,*
> *Your thoughts become your words,*
> *Your words become your actions,*
> *Your actions become your habits,*
> *Your habits become your values,*
> *Your values become your destiny.*

5. THE FIRST HORSEMAN OF ACCOMPLISHMENT: *PERSISTENCE*

> *Nothing in this world can take place of persistence. Talent will not; nothing is more common than an unsuccessful people with talent. Genius will not; unrewarded genius is almost a proverb. Education will not; the world is full of educated derelicts. Persistence and determination alone are omnipotent.*
>
> CALVIN COOLIDGE

Success is simply *not* possible without effort. Persistent effort. We have all thought about quitting when the going gets tough, however, the difference between those who achieve their dreams -- at least some of their dreams -- and those who don't is persistence. I found a way to attend St. Norbert College, my undergraduate alma mater, only days before classes started, after researching and calling 149 other colleges. Had I given up even a week earlier, who knows what my life would have been like? Persistence comes naturally to me. However, I love to use the example of my college search because it turned out well, and it took place during a very difficult year of my life.

When I came to the United States, I was to complete my

senior year as an exchange student at Greenfield High School and live with my sister's in-laws, who generously agreed to serve as my host family. I also had an exchange program coordinator, a lady who volunteered her time to place students into a good family, coordinate with the school, and keep tabs on students to make sure they are doing well. She was a wonderful source of support and a great human being. Both the coordinator and the family were helping students voluntarily; they received no compensation for their effort, and I will forever be grateful for their hospitality and patience.

That year was very transformative in many ways. Beyond my college hunt, I experienced my first Thanksgiving and Christmas in America; I had my first dream all in English and had a few crushes; I volunteered for the school newspaper, tried out for the school play, and attended a lot of basketball games. I went to prom (but found the experience displeasing). My access to Internet was limited to a few hours after school while my host mom was out, and I used that time to respond to emails and look for colleges. As the second semester rolled around, my college search intensified, particularly after I realized that I had missed a lot of deadlines.

The college application process in Europe starts a lot later than in the United States, so without a clear understanding on how it works here, I procrastinated. A part of me wishes that I hadn't; the other part is grateful that I did because it has brought me where I am today. There was also FAFSA (more on that in a later chapter) that I knew nothing about, in part because, as an international person, I was not eligible for it. Then came the ACT exam; I studied roughly a week and scored 26. Not an impressive score for a guy who otherwise spotted a high GPA and needed a very high score to win scholarships. But, given how late I was in the application process, I had no time to waste; some score was better than no score at all.

Since the time I checked out the first university, until I

enrolled at St. Norbert in August of 2005, I researched, explored, contacted -- often more than once -- and/or applied to 150 colleges and universities across the United States. From New York to Hawaii, from Georgia to Utah, I was searching for a school that would recognize my potential and would offer a financial aid package that would cover everything: tuition, room, and board. I couldn't pay application fees, either, so before I applied to some of the schools, I actually spent time writing emails asking them to waive the fee. Some places took me seriously; others laughed at me; and some ignored the fact that I was broke. I considered community colleges, vocational schools, religiously affiliated, private and public universities, although I did not quite understand the difference between all of them.

Nevertheless, I was very methodical in my process: I had a list of several hundred colleges, organized by state, and I went alphabetically. I was determined to call every one of them until someone responded positively. My logic was simple: out of thousands of colleges in the United States, I only needed one. That one first turned out to be Carroll College, now Carroll University, in Waukesha, WI. As the academic year was ending, I needed to enroll in a college that gave me the highest scholarship. This was Carroll. I accepted their offer and, thanks to my cousin's wife who offered to write a guarantee letter of support, I was able to demonstrate that I had sufficient funds to pay for college. Without this letter, they would have not allowed me to enroll or issue appropriate visa documents. Mom and Dad took out a loan back in Montenegro to try to help as well.

After talking to my admission counselor, I was under the impression that I could speak to various people once on campus in the Fall and try to secure additional funds beyond the first semester. I knew I had no money even for that first semester, but I went ahead with it because I needed to buy time. From there on, I was either going to find a different school that would help me more, or I would enroll at Carroll and then find alternatives while there. Over the summer I lived with my sister and brother-in-law and I spent a lot of time searching for alternatives. I am not sure either of them believed I would find a solution, but I was fortunate to have a roof above my head and use their old computer to keep pushing ahead.

At the end of July, as I kept crossing names off the list, I saw St. Norbert again. Namely, I was accepted and offered an international student scholarship, but this was not nearly enough to cover all expenses. However, I remembered the Dean of Admission talking about a priest who might be able to help. So, I decided to call again, only to be told that the Dean had left the college and a new person was in his place. It was this experience, along with many others since, that confirmed my belief that life works in mysterious ways and that things do happen for a reason. The new person called me back and, as I began spewing out all of my accomplishments, she simply asked: what is your need? The next day, I heard back from her and was given an offer that included the help from the Norbertine Order of Catholic Priests. I had no idea who these guys were, or how influenced I would become by the values of their founder, Norbert of Xanten, but I was beyond grateful and thrilled.

There was a catch though: a part of the offer was an anticipation that I would get a resident assistant position my sophomore year, which would help pay for the remaining years by covering my housing and meals. Otherwise, I would be short some $8,000-10,000, annually. Convinced that this wouldn't be a problem (how wrong I was!), I accepted the offer. Two weeks later I moved into my temporary housing in the basement of one of the dorms at St. Norbert. The money struggles weren't over, but I had a new home for the moment.

Before this experience, persistence was something I did intuitively. Since then, persistence has become a conscious effort. Yet, I am only a very small fish in the sea of people whose persistence defied their odds, enabling them to achieve the unachievable.

One of the best and most famous examples of unwavering persistence is that of Abraham Lincoln, the 16th President of the United States. Although quite popularized, Lincoln's journey to the White House is less known compared to his remarkable and transformational leadership during the very trying years of the American republic. His tragic end at the hands of John Wilkes Booth added to the ethos of the Great Emancipator, but it is the life he led and the trials he triumphed over that continue to inspire, 150 years after his death.

Born in Kentucky, Lincoln came from humble beginnings. The loss of his mother at the age of nine foreshadowed the many challenges and many defeats he was to face. With no formal schooling, his road to prominence was a steep one. His various business dealings resulted in failures and significant debt early on; his first try for public office in Illinois in 1832 was also a failure. His love for reading and passion for the law, however, allowed him to study informally and pass the bar in 1836. He persevered in his public office pursuits, ran again in 1834, and won, serving four consecutive terms. He was also elected to the U.S. House of Representatives for one term, but ended up losing his re-election and two separate bids for a U.S. Senate seat.

His personal dealings were equally as challenging; his sweetheart Ann Rutledge died shortly after their engagement (this was years before he married Mary Todd). There have been speculations about his sexuality, which at the time was beyond discussion for anyone, much less a public official, suggesting added inner troubles for the young statesman.

Below is a chronological list of Lincoln's journey. Various historians have debated its merits, and how certain events came about, however, one thing is clear: Mr. Lincoln's persistence and perseverance saw him through.

In the words of his law partner, "[Lincoln's] ambition was a little engine that knew no rest."

1818 – Lincoln's mother died
1832 – Lost job
1832 – Defeated for Illinois Legislature
1833 – Failed in business dealings
1834 – Elected to Illinois Legislature
1835 – Sweetheart Ann Rutledge died
1836 – Suffered a nervous breakdown
1838 – Defeated for Assembly Speaker
1840 – Defeated in becoming an elector
1843– Defeated in seeking a nomination for U.S. Congress
1846 – Elected to the U.S. House of Representatives
1848 – Lost re-election
1849 – Rejected for Land Officer position
1854 – Defeated in the election for the U.S. Senate
1856 – Lost nomination for Vice Presidency
1858 – Defeated in the election for the U.S. Senate
1860 – Elected President of the United States

As demonstrated by my own example, it is not only famous people who succeed thanks to their persistence. There are countless regular people whose stories we might never know, but whose perseverance allowed them to defy the odds and achieve at least some of their dreams.

In fact, I am willing to bet that you too can find at least one example in your own life where persistence decided the outcome. Can you think of one? Even the smallest examples of persistence (such as solving a math problem or winning a level in a computer game, not giving up until you figure it out) demonstrate one's character. And that characteristic is one you want to seize and build upon.

Think about instances of persistence in your own life. Are you a persistent person? If not, why would you quit before you succeed? There's an old saying that you are never defeated until you quit.

I think that is true.

6. THE OTHER THREE HORSEMEN:
PERSEVERANCE,
PATIENCE
PASSION

*Patience and perseverance have a magical effect
before which difficulties disappear and obstacles
vanish.*

JOHN QUINCY ADAMS

Persistence is the first of the "Four Horsemen of Accomplishment;" the other three are: perseverance, patience, and passion. Each is equally important in our ability to reach our dreams, build lasting relationships, achieve our goals, and live our best lives. Some would argue that persistence and perseverance are one and the same, but I have a slightly different understanding: persistence is active, it means we are trying to reach a goal; perseverance is more passive, it means we are not giving up.

Persistence equates to a polite aggression in the pursuit of a particular objective. In basketball, for example, we may miss a shot, but we keep taking shots until we score. Our persistence is what keeps us going when we have the energy; however, it is our perseverance that prevents us from quitting when we are out of breath. Persistence pushes us to play the game and fight for a trophy, but it is our persistence that keeps us playing the sport even when we lose.

Perseverance means that we don't give up when life gets really hard. If you can, try to imagine an 18-year-old immigrant with a fairly thick accent cold calling and emailing admission counselors asking for an opportunity to attend their college and offering hard work and commitment, and zero dollars; then hearing a "no" more than 140 times. I am not trying to sound flippant, but if I did it, you can too.

Perseverance also means standing by your principles even as your wellbeing is threatened and your basic survival endangered. For example, during my years as the executive editor of the *St. Norbert Times,* an independent college newspaper, we encountered a lot of opposition from administration. They could not understand why we would focus on the negative events on campus, instead of only writing about all that was positive. In our minds, our work was betting the community and, after all, we were in the business of pursuing and reporting the truth even if some people would not like it.

When a vice president was placed on leave without a solid explanation or a chance to offer the other side of the story, when three psychologists/counselors were let go in the span of 90 minutes, and when fundraising numbers were not adding up, we could not sit on our hands. This pursuit, however, came with a price. To protect my writers, I was often a target of these attacks. However, I knew that I had to find a way to persevere even in the face of highly inappropriate threats and behavior from the administration. As always, this was only possible because of others who stepped in to protect us as we learned how to be good journalists while doing it. We also called upon the moral superiority and obligations embedded in the Norbertine traditions and the First Amendment to the United States Constitution. These moral obligations are what fed our soul and fueled the flames of courage and perseverance.

Perseverance is sticking to your guns even as more comfortable options present themselves. Perseverance is when you feel lonely and rejected, because you may have been cheated on or your friends proved disloyal, yet you still find the strength to get up, brush yourself off, and keep going forward believing that loving and loyal relationships are possible for you.

On the other hand, patience means that we can step back, observe the circumstances, alter our approach, and not get frustrated along the way. Patience means that we know when to persistently poke at the issue and when to step back, licking our wounds and re-assessing the situation, before we go at it again. Patience isn't the same as waiting; the former is the state of trust, the latter the state of anxiousness. Patience is waiting for a donor to reply favorably to your letter requesting funding while remaining calm and thinking of other creative ways to pay your bills and continue the work of your social impact venture. Waiting, on the other hand, induces anxiety and paralyzes us from enjoying the present moment and coming up with alternative solutions. Patience means that we trust the process; that we know the difference between active persisting and passive persevering, while believing wholeheartedly that the best is indeed yet to come. Being patient is tough, because it requires us to let go of a desire for control and trust the final outcome. I have had a hard time with this, but every time I embraced patience, it paid off.

Finally, Mr. Coolidge was right in observing that persistence and determination alone are omnipotent. However, persistence, perseverance, and patience are fairly useless without passion. We cannot find the motivation to persistently pursue our goals, the strength to persevere when things get difficult, or the patience to watch it all unfold unless we *care*. Unless that something, or that someone, is important enough to us -- unless we are passionate -- it is not natural that we would have what it takes to persist, persevere, and remain patient. With that said, when you pick a goal, a project, a cause, or a person to pursue, make sure it is something that really matters to you. Otherwise, it will be wasted time. On the other hand, if you are passionate, do not hesitate to go forward because when we want something badly, and are willing to put in the work, the Universe conspires to help us.

Don't believe me?

Come up with a reasonable goal that is rooted in your passion, commit to it, set your mind on pursuing it…and see what happens.

7. SERVING THE WORLD

*No one cares how much you know until they
know how much you care.*
THEODORE ROOSEVELT

I loved many of the classes I took over the years, but the most rewarding experiences of my high school, college, and post-graduate careers happened through my involvement with various extracurricular activities, organizations, and service to my community. In fact, it is through that involvement that I found opportunities and was challenged to learn and grow. For example, in college, classes are essential to your academic success, because, after all, colleges are academic institutions. However, all that knowledge has its limits unless it is shared with and for the benefit of others.

My earliest involvement in the community began in Middle School, when I found myself writing a single edition of *The School Moth* news magazine. Although rejected, it empowered me to remain involved, speak up, and make a difference. This sense of empowerment led to my later involvement with high school Youth Parliaments, an initiative advocated for and supported by the United Nation's Children's Fund (UNICEF).

An equivalent to student governments elsewhere, Youth

Parliaments were designed to engage high school students in a democratic process of campaigning and running for office and voting for class representatives. Those elected would then have the opportunity to voice the needs and wants of their peers and work on improving the conditions at the school.

To put things in perspective, our schools only had white walls, wooden tables and chairs, unkempt hardwood floors, and a blackboard; there was only one classroom with several computers. Many teachers were tough graders who believed in perfection (one such teacher required us to know every capital city in the world or we failed the class) and a few would even get violent with students, yelling and even hitting a student. Standing up to teachers was not recommended and often punishable. Organized sports and clubs were not part of the curriculum, and education was based, for the most part, on outdated curricula.

Thankfully, there was a movement to change much of this and a lot was done through Youth Parliaments. For example, we worked to offer after-class activities by organizing sporting events, plays, workshops, HIV/AIDS and Drug Abuse awareness campaigns, and we also played music on class breaks. I was especially proud of being a "DJ" once a week, playing the classics such as Fugees' "Killing me Softly," Dolly Parton's "Jolene," Elvis Presley's "Always on My Mind," and my all-time favorite -- Charlie Daniels's "Devil Went Down to Georgia." What a mix!

We also worked with school administrators to empower our peers and give a voice to a generation of high school students whose childhood was interrupted with years of bloody wars, crime, and poverty. We succeeded at getting two student representatives on the school board and played a critical role during a teacher strike opposing the government's changes in the academic schedule. Finally, we wrote grants in order to win money from UNICEF and others to fund projects at the school. We truly made a difference, and it was during my sophomore year of high school that I landed my first business card: "President, Youth Parliament" it read below my name. I was proud.

My involvement in Youth Parliaments further led to my participation in the United Nations Eight Millennium Development Goals conference, and the work of the Organization for Security and Cooperation in Europe (OSCE), Local Democracy Agency (LDA), and CHF International (now Global Communities) all of which were aimed at empowering young people to better their lot and that of their fellow humans. It was at this same time that I also completed the School of Social Entrepreneurship, a multi-week program sponsored by the Norwegian Nansen Dialogue Centre, getting the first theoretical understanding of what it means to devote oneself to the betterment of the world while still enjoying a good life and having fun along the way.

Upon my arrival in the United States, and later in college, I spent much of my time volunteering in various capacities.

Following in the tradition of the Norbertine Fathers, the founders and guardians of my undergraduate alma mater, St. Norbert College placed a great emphasis on service to others. I took this seriously and over my four years there I served on twelve standing committees of the college, including representing students with the Board of Trustees. I was elected Secretary and Vice President of Student Government, and was a member of the National Residence Hall Honorary, Residence Hall Association, Pi Sigma Alpha political science honor society, and Phi Beta Delta international honor society. I served nearly four years as President of Beyond Borders, a diversity organization that worked to challenge students to go beyond their cultural and personal borders by learning, sharing, and communicating with people from different backgrounds, and I also found Global Scholars international studies academic organization during my senior year. This was a lot.

One of the most rewarding, and perhaps most challenging experiences during my college years, was my time as Editor of the *St. Norbert Times* student newspaper. At a college without a journalism program, running a newspaper was placed on the shoulders of student volunteers. When I became editor my junior year, the newspaper was rarely published and had two other staff members. In the two years that followed, we built a newspaper into a respected, well designed and regularly published publication with over 50 staff members and readership that spiked from several dozen to several thousand.

We also pursued stories with polite aggression which, as I mentioned, often infuriated many members of the college's administration. At one particularly hairy occasion, a member of the college's Board of Trustees told me, "I want to grab you and smack you through that window," because she did not like the story we were working on about the college's presidential search. At another similar occasion, through careful politicking, a former administrator stripped me from a scholarship and later threatened my expulsion because I directed my staff to go after "touchy" subjects.

Those experiences were powerful and transformative. They challenged me to stand by my values, persevere, and have the courage to withstand the pressure. And they would not have necessarily happened in the safe confines of a classroom. Thankfully, through the Norbertine commitment to justice, the encouragement of the Faculty and the community at large, and the incredible courage, hard work, and dedication of my team, we prevailed and were affirmed in our conviction to follow the truth no matter where it led. The college's next president turned out to be a former journalist!

Many opportunities to serve came after college, too, and I am grateful for each one of them.

I share these experiences with you, not to brag about all that I have done, because there are many people who have done a lot more, and I probably sound like a hopeless overachiever anyway. Rather, I share that to demonstrate the variety of opportunities for service, my own credibility in speaking about it and the impact it can have on you, and to make one critical point: the time is always right to get involved and contribute to the greater good of all.

When you take the time from your day to get involved with clubs at your school, partake in sports, and/or go out and serve others through a local organization or volunteer center, church, masque, synagogue, or temple, many new opportunities will present themselves. You will meet new people and new doors will open, your resume will lengthen through a myriad of internships, jobs, and invitations to serve, and you will demonstrate your concern for people's well being and for the society.

What is more, you will make a difference in the lives of others.

This latter one, more than anything else, will inform and transform your life. Standing up for others in need, especially those experiencing injustice, is powerfully transformative to you and to the society. It also shows that you care. And once people see that you do care -- in both word and deed -- they will be delighted to return the favor and care about you. And they will do so by helping you during the times of need, writing recommendations, connecting you with the right people, and simply being there for you when you need them. They will also be more tolerant when you make mistakes, and -- in terms of academics -- a B+ can often become an A when teachers see your capacity inside and outside the classroom. Many professors were beyond understanding and supportive during my work with *the Times*.

Of course, if you are getting Ds, service to your community won't earn you As. It also won't pay your bills. Or, if it is clear that you are volunteering with an expectation of getting something in return, you will burn yourself. If you take my advice and help people by getting involved in your community, do it because *you* want to. And no matter how much time you spend, make sure that the time you do devote comes from a genuine place.

Finally, no matter how small or large your contribution may seem, the act of selfless giving is good for your soul. It is self-validating and a boost to your self-esteem. It is a source of happiness.

~

The first step in serving others begins with figuring out what you like doing so that you can match your passions with the need and the appropriate organizations.

If you have been successful in finding your passion and discovering your purpose, through the exercises offered in the earlier chapter, then you will know exactly where to look for service opportunities. If you haven't gotten there yet (or you skipped the chapter altogether), here are some questions you might want to ask as a way of understanding what you like and what cause may best suit you: *Have you ever stood up to a bully? Would you do it in the future?* If so, that's a good sign that you are proactive in fighting for other people's rights. Perhaps you can find an organization that does this in some way. *Do you enjoy crafting? What about signing or playing a music instrument? What about animals or children? Do you attend religious services? What about the elderly? What about your career's professional development organization? What about a hobby you had in childhood? Is there any way that you can connect the hobby with your present-day skills, and tie all that into putting it to work for a good cause? Are there professional organizations or associations you believe in and want to contribute to, even though their field has nothing to do with yours?*

The list of questions is endless. Try to answer some of these honestly in order to figure out what you enjoy and then find a list of organizations at your school or in your community and see which ones speak to you. In general, nonprofit organizations *love* people eager to get involved. They will love you too as long as your dedication and desire to get involved are genuine and your commitment certain.

In working with volunteers for years now, I have come to believe that they are the greatest assets of any organization. However, I also have found that holding volunteers accountable, as if they were paid, is as important as is inspiring them with your organization's mission or leadership style. I am a big proponent of "firing" volunteers if they don't perform, just like I encourage people to *always* say "no" if they don't want to do something. In my experience, what often happens is that people sign up to volunteer even though they'd rather be doing something else. This approach leaves everyone dissatisfied, time is wasted, and the work doesn't get done.

So, if you are thinking about making a difference in the lives of others through volunteering, spend time discovering your passions and finding a cause that is the right fit. Volunteering does not only mean going to a soup kitchen; there are many ways to contribute. For example, for the last few years, I have served on several committees of the American Library Association. I am not a librarian, but believe in their cause and the work entails a lot of reading, writing, and many meetings. No soup kitchens or puppies, but it still makes a difference. With that said, be honest with yourself and others. That will save you headaches later on and make your volunteering experience truly rewarding.

ADI REDZIC

PART TWO
Relationships

8. RELATIONSHIP CIRCLES

> *Man is by nature a social animal; an individual*
> *who is unsocial naturally and not accidentally is*
> *either beneath our notice or more than human.*
> *Society is something that precedes the individual.*
> *Anyone who either cannot lead the common life,*
> *or is so self-sufficient as not to need to, and*
> *therefore does not partake of society, is either*
> *beast or a god.*
> ARISTOTLE

It is always about relationships.

Relationships define and enhance our journey through life, both personal and professional, and they color all of our interactions: those at work, school, boardroom, and a drive-thru. Psychotherapist C. G. Jung observed that the meeting of two personalities is like the contact of two chemical substances: if there is any reaction, both are transformed. The depth of relationship determines the depth of transformation.

This is true for all of our relationships.

It is said that people come into our lives for a reason, a season, or a lifetime. Each of those people teaches us something, either about the world, or ourselves, and they help us move along our life's journey. It is through these relationships that we are able to grow. Even the most introverted among us need human connection to make life meaningful. Furthermore, none of us got anywhere in life without the help of others: pretending that we did is arrogant and trying to do it alone is foolish. In other words, to live -- and especially to live well -- we need other people. We need relationships to thrive.

In writing this book, I felt compelled to dedicate a few passages to relationships. Countless books have been written specifically on this topic that offer a more comprehensive take on this large, complex, and often complicated topic. However, relationships have been instrumental in my life: had it not been for other people, I would have never been where I am today. I fell in love with reading and writing thanks to Vera, a family friend from childhood. My college education and graduate school were made possible by the support and generosity of several incredible individuals whose faith in me motivated me -- and continues to motivate me -- to pursue my dreams, do better, and make the world a little better, too. I landed my first job thanks to a mentor. I entered the world of financial security thanks to a former professor and ventured onto the national stage in empowering my generation, thanks to another very close friend of mine. Any successful project I ever attempted involved others. The list goes on.

All along, I have also been blessed by the people who believed in me even when I didn't, and who stood by me through thick and thin; people who mentored me, taught me, and offered their love and support -- and bailed me out from several very tough situations.

Just like anyone else, I too have had disappointments and times when I cursed relationships. I have been screwed over, cheated on, left to hang dry, fired, endured a bad boss, and been hated for my ambition, my background, or my demeanor. As a result, I felt lonely, unloved, and deeply rejected. These feelings come to most of us at one point. For others, these moments happen more often than they are willing to admit. The fact is, people are fundamentally good.

And even though we all encounter some a-holes in our lives, that does not diminish all the good that happened to us because of others.

I like to think that those who hurt me came into my life for a reason, some stayed for a season, but only the best ones will stay for a lifetime. It is the good ones that we need to focus on, give them the care and nurturing they deserve, and let them into our inner "relationship circles." The others are, ultimately, irrelevant.

For me, relationships fall into a series of concentric circles, each playing a particular role in our lives. There are inner circles -- those closer to us -- and the outer ones. The reason for having these circles is because they help us manage our relationships; our expectations, our commitments, and our time. They are not cut and dry, and this method has different facets, depending on a particular situation. However, in general, I have found circles useful in helping me understand my relationships and find clarity:

1. First Circle includes you, your creator, and perhaps another human being. This is the most sacred space, one that needs to be safe and secure. If you are sharing it with someone, that person is your partner in crime and you take on the world together. Nurturing and nourishing this circle takes most time and effort. Conversely, if this circle isn't in order or if it gets disrupted, it has a domino effect in harming all other circles.

2. Second Circle closely follows the first one and includes 1-5 of our closest friends, confidants, family members, or mentors. If you are very lucky, it may include a few more. This group is unequivocally trusted, you communicate frequently, have honest conversations and are there for each other. If you don't have this group, you want to build it. Odds are, however, that you probably do and that you just haven't thought of them in these terms.

3. Third Circle includes people who are close, trustworthy and trusting, but who did not make the cut to fall into the second circle. They often include mentors that you may not talk to often, or friends who you know are there for you but not in touch as frequently as you'd like. People in the second and third circles can, and often do, switch places. This is the last circle that falls under the umbrella of "inner circles."

4. Fourth Circle includes mentors, advisors, supporters, distant friends and relatives, and those people that you feel connected to in some way, but may not have a consistent relationship with and you may not know everything about each other. This circle also represents individuals who have affected your life in a meaningful way, helped you at some point, and for whom you feel a sense of loyalty and allegiance.

5. Fifth Circle includes your classmates, co-workers, and people that you interact with, people that you know, and occasionally exchange pleasantries or work with to some degree but don't feel deep connection to. These are your Facebook friends and LinkedIn connections. You wish well for each other, but if you were in trouble, you probably would not think to call people in this circle.

6. Sixth Circle includes everyone else that you know and connect with.

My relationship circles remind me of Robert DeNiro's "trust circle" from "Meet the Parents" movie. Trust is essential for healthy and lasting relationships. However, trust is a two-way street. It takes one to be trustworthy in order to be trusted. Likewise, we need to trust in order to allow people to show us that they are trustworthy. It is the chicken-egg dynamic. In any event, without trust -- at some level -- no genuine relationship is possible.

To obtain trust, however, we need vulnerability. Why would people trust someone who is phony and dishonest, someone unable to share what they think or feel? Vulnerability means that we open to people; that we express our sincere emotion and that we show the rawness of our soul. Personally, I love people who have the courage to show me their soul. We are too often guarded and fearful. This is understandable because being vulnerable is very difficult. It is also very scary. But without it, no meaningful relationship is possible. Which is also why we need to find a way to allow other people to feel safe around us, so that they can be vulnerable, and make ourselves trustworthy so that we can be trusted.

Even though relationships play such an important role in our lives, study after study suggests that loneliness is the disease for the 21st century in much of the western world. We count our Facebook friends, text, and post Instagram images while our sense of isolation grows. We collect business cards and sing praise to "networking," yet we make few deep and lasting connections. Instead of picking up the phone, we "like" a status. We keep sharing information and ideas instead of creating new ones or, even better, sharing our true feelings. Social media outlets allow us to express personas that we create as a ploy of getting instant validation, which has its merits, but it also places us in a precarious position where our rawness falls by the wayside. We depend on the gadgets so much that instead of staying present in the moment, enjoying our food or conversation, we take breaks to "check-in" or post a selfie. Instead of making plans to take a road trip and see our friends, we spend hours consuming information that does little to enrich our life in a meaningful way, but does a lot to clutter it. We are more connected than ever, yet we are lonelier than ever.

I myself am a victim of this pattern. I checked my Facebook page at least two times while writing this chapter. I wrote a post about Joan Rivers' passing and sent a couple messages. The irony is obvious. The fact remains, however, that our instant connectedness is wonderful in its way because it allows us to communicate at a much greater speed, create and share information with others all around the world, and makes our lives more entertaining and interesting, cat videos and all. The trick is to understand the trap that it represents and to find the discipline to focus on our actual life, not fantasy; real relationships, not fabrications of our imagination; and use the internet to improve our lot, and that of others, instead of living lives that are out of touch. I fear that the virtual world will take us so far from reality that we will wake up one day and not recognize ourselves. There's a great saying attributed to Edward Norton, "Instead of telling the world what you are eating for breakfast, you can use social networking to do something that's meaningful."

I encourage you to step back and see if you can fill circles with real people. Take a few moments of silence every day to step back from the distractions in order to feel awake and alive. Feel your heartbeat. Take a few deep breaths. Ask yourself how many friends would you actually have -- and communicate with -- if Facebook weren't there. Give a call to someone you haven't talked to in a while. Write a letter expressing your emotion, your gratitude. Tell those around you that you love them: be raw with them, share your fears and struggles.

Relationship Circles are meant to help us see who is really important in our life and to give us the discipline to cherish few real, authentic relationships, as opposed to growing hundreds or thousands of limited, shallow ones. Time we have on this earth is finite and trying to be loved -- even liked -- by our acquaintances is a futile and foolish business. Having lots of friends, even more connections, might sound great, but is very difficult to attain and, ultimately, is not fulfilling. When it comes to genuine relationships, our time constraints (and personal likes and dislikes) limit us to a select few. These circles can help you find clarity and make those few count..

9. WHO WILL RIDE THE BUS?

Lots of people want to ride with you in the limo,
but what you want is someone who will take the
bus with you when the limo breaks down.
OPRAH WINFREY

Who are the people who would ride the bus with you today?

Growing up, we are often taught lessons about life that are rooted in our parents' experiences and the communal or societal norms. However, these vary significantly from one another, and the lessons my parents taught me aren't necessarily the lessons you learned. Or the lessons your next-door neighbor learned.

What this means is that we grow up developing certain expectations, and these expectations in turn inform our view of the world and our decisions. Often, we emulate our parents or other adults in our lives, and think the world has to be the way they told us it is. This is a natural process. It is also a flawed one, because it prevents us from growing up to use our own heads for thinking and making sense of the world based on our own feelings, experiences, understandings, *and* dreams.

For example, you may think that it is the responsibility of

your family or of the government to pay for your education. Or perhaps you feel like you can't achieve much in life because of where you were born, your life's circumstances, and the people you know (or don't know). Maybe you are urged to follow in the footsteps of your parents and feel horrible when you don't, or you compete with your siblings and feel inadequate when they are better at something than you. It is only when we drop these views that our authentic pursuit of happiness is possible.

When I first came to the United States, my sister and brother were already here. They had come eight and six years earlier, respectively. They both completed their college degrees several years earlier and were working. Then, there was my sister's husband and their dog Maggie, a one-year-old Jack Russell Terrier who terrorized everyone. I reunited with several of my cousins and met their wives, boyfriend, and children. My uncle was here at that time, too. But, as time went by, something strange happened: I felt like an outsider. It was strange because I did not arrive *expecting* that I would be an outsider, but perhaps I was.

It is interesting how we may feel loyalty and allegiance to our family and cousins, yet feel profoundly disconnected and distant from them. In my case, I had underestimated what years of separation had done. I was 9 years old when my sister left, 11 when my brother left, and a lot younger when my cousins left. Although I had seen them since, and we had kept in touch, this was long before Skype, Facebook, and instant communication. We had each grown up independently, immersed in our own experiences -- both happy and sad -- and the connection that we maybe expected to have was not exactly there. At the same time, we all had certain *expectations* from each other, and had painted a picture of the other person based on our understanding of events and memories from a distance, or by looking through the lens offered by others.

For my part, I had hoped that they would understand me better than *I felt* they did. I expected they would know what was on my mind and how much I was struggling, that they would support me unconditionally, and wholeheartedly accept me as an addition to their lives. On their end, and I am just speculating, perhaps they wanted me to be less melancholic, less spoiled, more understanding of their own lives, to not make a fool of myself, and/or take their advice about how to do things. Of course, I rebelled. And instead of remaining open, creating a safe, nonjudgmental zone, and taking the time to get to know each other, we often anticipated how the other person might act. These expectations were tough, because disappointments were inevitable. I am told that this is the story of most families.

Much of this is water under the bridge today, but these experiences -- and those that followed -- taught me the importance of maintaining no expectations regarding others, including our families. A lot of people talk about the importance of family and relatives, and in theory these claims sound wonderful. However, in reality, they are generally based on personal views of the world, groupthink, past experiences, expectations, or how life "should be," and not agreed upon by both parties, as is usually the case in friendships or even romantic relationships. As my story revealed, in the years following my arrival, I met many people who have become incredibly close and supported me in various ways. Many of those individuals have become a part of my inner circles, and I feel deeply grateful for each of them. At the same time, after we found some distance and allowed each other to shine in our own light, my siblings and I also learned to appreciate and support each other more, without the interference of personal expectations.

. These experiences have taught me that relationships of any kind can be successful only when we learn to respect each other for who we are and drop expectations that either of us would be or should be any different. When we do this, in *all* relationships, we allow the other person to level with us genuinely, thus opening doors to form authentically meaningful relationships because we want to, not because we feel we should.

In figuring out who would ride the bus with us, and who we would ride with, we need to focus on riding our own bus and clarifying our values – once again, what is important to us -- and discover our passions and purpose. As the ride continues, the people who need to be on our bus will join for a reason, season, or a lifetime. Their values and desires will align with ours and vice versa.

It is too often that people live their lives trying to fit the mold of a society and people around us. Back in the day when staying within a tribe was necessary for survival, it made sense. But as we continue to evolve, and personal self-esteem and self-actualization take a more prominent role in our life, listening to our own call is more important than ever.

So often, we develop a belief that people should have certain reactions to us. Help us. Not help us. Support us. Love us. But thinking this way is a futile endeavor, because we have no control over other people's feelings or actions. What we can do, however, is let go of expectations we hold, be ourselves, and trust. I understand that this is much easier said than done. We are uncomfortable with struggle, and try to avoid it. Most of us want things to simply happen for us and when they don't, we are inclined to blame others. This process is useless. Blaming, complaining, being upset -- at the end of the day, all of it matters little.

These are tips that I try to stick to, and that have helped me figure out who is on my bus, which bus I need to join, and how to create a support network:

1. Build your own family. One of my favorite films is *The Godfather.* While Coppola's masterpiece is spectacular for many reasons, one particular lesson resonates: build your own family. Bring together a family that includes people who love and support you for who you are. They do so because they want to, not because they have to, and they don't ask you to change. You know how there are people in your life that you like and simply want them to be happy? There are others out there who feel that way about you. They can be related to you or not, but they will represent your own family nevertheless. And don't focus on the people who don't support you. As a former mentor of mine once said, "no matter what you do, one-third of people will love you, one-third will dislike you, and the rest will be indifferent." Unless you are running for a political office, focus on the first one-third. This is where positivity, encouragement, and solutions will come from.

2. Clearly understand what people will do for you. For example, when I was figuring out college, I spoke with my parents and asked how much they could help. I knew they would do the best they could, but their best was not going to be enough to take me through college. Later on, I would write down all expected sources of income, so that I could have a clear picture of the gap, and focus on bridging it. This goes back to the principles of responsibility. This translates into expectations. By asking honest questions, we clarify expectations and know where everyone stands.

3. Look for affinity in people. Learn about people as much as you can, because their stories will tell you if the two of you are compatible, or if there's really no future in your relationship (friendship, and otherwise). It is often people who carry similar burdens and similar pains that can best understand each other. Those are affinities that bring and tie them together. It is shared values that create a bond and keep people together. I think it was Charlie Brown who said, as you get older you will realize that you don't need to have many friends, you just need a few good ones.

4. Do not waste your time living other people's understanding of life. Do not let the chatter of naysayers and other people's opinions drown out your inner voice and the cheering of those who do support you. Even if it seems like no one is in your corner at the moment, trust your gut. Your intuition, that little feeling that tells you "this feels right," will never lead you astray. Don't mistake it for fear, however; intuition is never fear. The only regret we might have down the road won't be that we tried and failed, but that we never tried. I would have *never* been here had I listened to those who doubted my GPA, my dreams, my interests, and my passions. Even when those closest to you doubt you, don't let them kill your spirit.

5. Get down from your high horse of ego-driven pride and ask for help. It's up to them to say "yes" or "no"; don't blame them if they say "no." Focus on someone who will say "yes."

6. Do not play a victim. All these lessons go back to that first one: responsibility is key. Take responsibility for your life.

10. NETWORKING

Personal relationships are always the key to good business. You can buy networking; you can't buy friendships.
LINDSAY FOX

"It is not what you know, but who you know." The old adage is true, but knowing someone -- especially in this day and age of social media -- does not mean you have a relationship that is mutually rewarding. Networking in the old-fashioned practice of exchanging business cards does not mean we are building a relationship. Adding someone on LinkedIn or following them on Twitter does not mean we have struck a friendship. We can only wish that effective networking was that easy! Instead, effective networking depends on several factors that transform networking as a buzz word into networking as a pathway to relationships. In my experience, most people network because that is just what you do; few are effective.

Another misconception about networking is the idea of six degrees of separation. That is to say, each of us is separated by six degrees from everyone else in the world. I do not believe this is true. I am a supporter of a theory that less than one third of people in this world are connected by six degrees from everyone else. And those select few are true

73

networkers.

There are many books written on networking, on how to connect with people, and I can list quite a few that I have read. However, I want to address several underlying premises behind networking that have served me well and I believe you will need in order to achieve success in any endeavor:

Give Value

I read somewhere that the best way to network is to come up with five ideas on how two people can help each other. Introduce them and get out of the way. This is how real networking is done: giving value to someone. Consider what you have to offer in terms of connections, energy, emotion, work, and so on and match that with someone else and the things they might want, need, or appreciate. This may be a fuzzy feeling, an introduction, an activity, or something else that a person needs. By doing so, you score a win-win situation.

Be Grateful and Stay Positive

One of the most powerful emotions is gratitude. In building relationships -- through networking or otherwise -- feel and express gratitude as often as you can. Say thank you. Write a thank you note. Show your gratitude through your words and deeds. It is this gratitude that will open doors and build relationships. People don't need to do magnificent things for us so that we can feel and be grateful. If you can have enough humility to be grateful for the little stuff, imagine how amazing the big stuff will feel. People will see and feel your gratitude. It will reflect as positivity.

Which is my second point: stay positive. Of course, we all have problems and we all like to complain about them. But, ask yourself, do you like to be around negative people? Neither do I. It is one thing if you struggle and share your problems with others, and do it as a matter of habit, but it is an entirely different thing if you are working toward resolving something as you are bitching about it. The latter is forgivable and it allows people to feel compassion. The former? That won't take you far, in life or in building relationships and networking.

There was a girl who was talented, had a great story, and many people wanted to help her. Except, she did not demonstrate any gratitude for all that people did do for her. Instead, she consistently complained. Result: people walked away from her. Life can be very tough, but if all you do is complain about it without taking action -- without owning it -- it will be even tougher because few people will want to engage with you.

When you are positive -- even optimistic about life -- and express gratitude for even the smallest of opportunities you have, people will be compelled to give a helping hand and advance you along. And, in networking, it is hard enough connecting with people as is. Being negative and ungrateful makes relationship prospects even harder.

Follow-up and Follow through

Meeting people and handing out business cards is pointless ... unless you follow up and find ways to develop a relationship. When meeting someone, try to go beyond the pleasantries and traditional "what do you do?" questions, and try to learn more about the people you are meeting. We all have stories, we all have emotions, and we all have histories. And we all like to share them. The more you can connect with people at a fundamental level and follow-up with them, the more likely you will be to form a relationship. You want to remember details from your conversations, so the next day or at some point in the future, you can follow up in a meaningful way. Even sending a handwritten card (or an email) that includes a mention of something from your conversation tells the other person that you are thoughtful and actually listened to them. Thoughtfulness goes a long way in cultivating and maintaining any relationship, regardless of the circle people are in.

Trust and Trustworthiness

Focus on building trust and making yourself trustworthy to the people you meet. First impressions are important, so make sure to leave a good one by looking and behaving professionally. Leaving a good first impression does not mean you should try to impress people; that can come across phony. Instead, just be you, stay positive, engaging, listen to others, and practice basic etiquette. When it comes to etiquette, one of my favorite quotes is: "When in Rome, do as Romans do." In other words, understand the setting you will be in and prepare yourself for it.

For example, when I was attending the St. Norbert College Board of Trustees dinner for the first time, I made sure to understand what the setting was going to be like, what the proper attire was. And I prepared for it by getting a suit and a tie, and reading up on proper dinner etiquette (e.g. which fork do I take first?). First impressions open doors for trust -- however, this does not mean you should be fake. Without sincerity, the first impression would have been simply a show, and people won't trust you the next day.

Trust is a fundamental building block of any relationship. In fact, without trust, no meaningful relationship is possible. We can have shallow and superficial relationships with many people -- and we often do -- but if we want to make a meaningful connection and allow people to enter our circles -- and us enter theirs -- we need to work on trust. Naturally, trust begins by us walking the talk and talking the walk; that is to say, trust begins with integrity. You want to say the truth, always, but beyond that, you also want to make sure that you live up to your own values, do the right thing even when it is hard – such as when no one is watching -- and demonstrate that you do indeed care about people (as opposed to pretending) and have enough courage to say that you don't if that is the case.

In the age when manipulation, marketing, and political divide are common, many have devalued the power and importance of our word and have jumped on the bandwagon of thinking that trust is neither common nor possible. The thing is, if we do not believe our word is sacred, why would we expect others to give us their word and stand by it?

Conversely, it is possible that we are consistent in standing behind our commitments and our word while others don't keep their part of the bargain. Many of us have been there, and those experiences hurt. Consequently, we begin to wonder if we should keep doing that because "it doesn't matter." But, it *does* matter. Our world has become more mistrusting and cynical. You may argue that we have plenty of reasons for it, and that I am idealistic to think we can place such value on trust, and I would agree with you. But if I cannot have enough idealism to strive to build relationships founded on trust, I have no place hoping to bring more peace and justice into the world. Trust starts with us. Self-trust, and trust in relation to others. You will be betrayed, lied to, cheated on, and screwed over. Be wise in judging people's character, but don't stop giving someone an opportunity until proven otherwise.

Finally, one of the best stories to illustrate the power of one's word was that of a business owner who planned to sell his company in two year's time. He found a buyer and they agreed on a price, shook hands on it and agreed to complete the transaction two years later. In the months following the handshake, the value of the company skyrocketed. As the purchase date neared, the buyer called up the seller and admitted that he could not afford to buy the new value of the company. The seller laughed and asked "What new value? We shook hands, didn't we? I am selling you my company at that price. My word is more important to me than money."

I hope you feel the same way. If you do, clear conscience will be yours.

One last thing

A last word on networking: it is not about networks, it is bout community. When we speak of networks, work to develop our own, and try to add people to it, a fundamental link is missing: emotion. Networks imply that they will take us somewhere; that we are connected so that we can achieve something. They are non-fluid. Often, they are one-directional. In comparison, communities are all about emotion. They include people that they have a touching point with us; they can relate to us and perhaps we share similar identities, backgrounds, values, and experiences -- and are fluid, collegial, collaborative, and imbued in emotion.

So, when considering networking and connecting with people, ask yourself: am I simply playing the game of networking, or am I open to adding this person into my community -- of friends, colleagues, business partners, and so on. When we don't cool down relationships through the cold business-card exchange, but warm them up with the idea of community, we are likely to spend time developing meaningful connections. It is those connections that ultimately benefit us far more than dozens of business cards. Social media and popular networking has a purpose; that purpose is sharing and exchanging information. Promote your work, brighten up someone's day, share information. If you want to build something meaningful, look at the individual, your community, and the relationships that comprise it.

11. MENTORING

If you cannot see where you are going, ask someone who has been there before.

J. LOREN NORRIS

I am blessed. And one of the greatest blessings in my life, since my childhood, has been people who have served as my mentors.

Although they *can* be, parents are often not mentors. The relationship is inherently different. Mentors exist to guide us, based on their own experience, as we navigate particular areas of life. Some mentors show up in college, others show up in our career. Some mentors stay for a long time , others come and go. Sometimes, we have a closer relationship with one mentor than another, and other times we have a falling out. In the best-case scenario, our mentors become our friends. I have been fortunate. I had a mentor who has been incredibly transformational for me, and I believe our bond will always be there, although our different approaches to life saw us distancing from each other. Another mentor from college is a very close friend, and our relationship has changed. It has grown from a mentor-to-mentee relationship into a peer-to-peer relationship.

The purpose of mentors is to help us navigate life. They

usually recognize themselves in us, or see potential within us, and they help cultivate that through objective feedback and honesty, encouragement, by opening doors, and sometimes by offering constructive criticism. Often, this relationship is one-sided, because the idea is that the mentor will teach the mentee all they know about a particular topic, area of life, work, and so on. Once the teaching moment has reached its zenith, if ever, the relationship needs to evolve into something else.

Many people feel they have nothing to share with others, so they shy away from being mentors. Conversely, many young people are ashamed to admit that they don't know it all, to be vulnerable, and to trust an older person to help them navigate. Don't be a fool. It does not matter how old or how young you are, we can all benefit by engaging in this relationship. Did you know that President George H. W. Bush mentored President Bill Clinton? Even though the latter beat the former for political office. Since leaving The White House, these two men also found a way to strike a friendship.

Mentors can play a critical role in offering honest, supportive and yet objective advice in all spheres of life. Mentors can connect us with the right people, and warn us about making a potentially stupid mistake. And mentoring someone can be incredibly rewarding. Not only are you paying it forward -- remembering all those that came before and mentored you -- but seeing a transformation in your mentee is tremendous. I encourage you to share your wisdom with others. Think of the incredible impact organizations that are based on mentoring have had on the lives of millions: Big Brothers Big Sisters, Boys and Girls Clubs, and so on. By making ourselves available to mentor those that are up and coming, and by seeking mentors to help us out, we are enriching each other's lives and everyone wins.

To find a mentor, ask for one by engaging them through questions about life or their craft. You can ask someone directly to mentor you. There are organizations that help match mentors and mentees. Career Services offices in colleges do this. Student life affairs staff, coaches, and librarians serve as wonderful mentors. Use social media to land a mentor. Resources are there -- you just have to ask.

To be a mentor, make yourself available. If you meet someone with potential, or someone you resonate with, see if you can develop a relationship. Show up at your local volunteer center, place of worship, or school. Post on social media that you are looking to mentor someone, or identify a person or two among your connections.

Let me lead by example: if you want me to mentor you, coach you -- or you want to be my mentor -- please contact me. I'd love to hear from you!

PART THREE
Learning

ADI REDZIC

12. LEARNING FOR
THE LOVE OF LEARNING

An investment in knowledge pays the best interest.
BENJAMIN FRANKLIN

As a high school student in the old country, as I mentioned, I was very involved with Youth Parliaments. It was during this time that I was first exposed to workshops on social entrepreneurship, communication, project management, and leadership. It was also then that one of our faculty advisors told me something that stuck: "knowledge is power." The more we know, the more powerful we are.

However, educational systems sometimes get caught up in the logistics and the outcomes of learning, instead of instilling a love of learning within us. They are often focused on the practicalities rather than the passions and thus use the "carrot and stick" principle to motivate us to learn. Instead of harnessing our curiosity and helping us understand how much richer our lives become through learning, we are often told that by doing well in school, and in particular subjects, we are offered more opportunities to achieve more schooling (e.g. doing well in high school will land you at a good college), and that this education will lead to a greater likelihood of prosperous and fulfilling lives. The opposite of an educational pursuit, the storyline goes, is lack of prosperity.

Except, this isn't always true.

Motivational blogs and self-help books are filled with stories of the unlikely achievers. Think of Steve Jobs. He dropped out of college, yet went on to co-found (and later save) one of the most innovative and most valued companies of our time, Apple Inc. What was rarely reported early on about Jobs is that he loved a calligraphy class he took in college. He relished it so much, and was so good at it, that he excelled in it. And, even though he dropped out of college shortly thereafter, those lessons acquired in that class were used later on to design various Apple products.

You can be a success without a college degree. However, you cannot be a success without a passion for learning.

To illustrate this point further, let's take a look at one of my favorite statesman: Benjamin Franklin. He was a printer, author, political theorist, politician, postmaster, scientist, inventor, community activist, founder of a university, statesman, and a diplomat. Yet, he barely had any formal education.

What these two men -- and thousands of others who have been able to lead fulfilling lives -- have in common is a desire to learn for the sake of learning. Jobs did not worry about his career prospects when he left college and ventured off to India. Franklin had no reason to play with electricity for work; he did it because he was curious. He wanted to know more. He wanted to discover something new.

When we study any topic, we follow our passion to discover something new. We do it because we enjoy it, not because we may get something in return (e.g. a job). And, if we are driven by our love for learning, when we encounter a topic we dislike or have a hard time grasping, we ask for help and put in the time necessary to master it at some level.

The opposite is true, too. When we feel we are going to school because "we have to," or are told we are stupid if we are slower at understanding a particular subject, we lose our curiosity and love for learning.

Once learning happens for the sake of learning, there are few dreams that we cannot chase. We are well rounded and able to engage in conversations and build relationships with diverse people. We are able to connect the dots in order to solve day-to-day problems. If nothing else, we are more interesting and life is more interesting.

I believe that education *is* the answer to all social and economic challenges of our time. So, I'm not saying that avoiding an education should ever be a choice. In fact, I think we should all get as much education as possible. It is true that with education often comes a greater earning power and a wider-array of opportunities. But if you can learn because you love learning, and pursue topics you are curious and passionate about, then in addition to societal advances, you will acquire unique personal power and fulfillment that only comes through knowledge and forever stays with you.

ADI REDZIC

13. FORMAL EDUCATION: DO YOU NEED IT?

> *A mind is a fire to be kindled,*
> *not a vessel to be filled.*
> PLUTARCH

Formal education, as we know it today, is a fairly new invention. For a long time in our human history, many people dreamed of attaining an education as a way of advancing in the society and bettering their lot. Even so, formal education remained a privilege bestowed upon a select few who could afford it. It wasn't until after the Industrial Revolution that this began to change and schooling became accessible to and sometimes mandatory for the masses. In the West, college education came into prominence after World War II, leading to the rise of the "white collar" job. And in the decades to follow, especially in the United States, college education became a status symbol; a guarantee of sorts that you would have a well-paying job and a bright future.

Over the last couple of decades, however, more people began to question the value of formal education. Is college worth the expense? According to several studies, including the one by iOme Challenge, most people still think it is, but it is no surprise that many more are less convinced. As we observe Steve Jobs, Bill Gates, Mark Zuckerberg, and others who dropped out of college in the pursuit of their dreams, and made it big -- and as tuition and fees continue to increase exponentially while our salaries remain stagnant and jobs scarce -- it is natural that many of us begin to wonder if we should bother.

Another aspect is that often, we haven't a clue what we want to do when we grow up. So, we spend four years and thousands of dollars studying something that we may not even use. We acquire skills that may seem obsolete too soon, and acquire debt that burdens us for too long.

As we contemplate these realities, and as we deliberate if we should go to college at all, or go back to school to shore up our skills or pursue an advanced degree, the vista is muddy. Fundamentally, this confusion has to do with our lack of understanding about what an education is really for. We have been socialized into thinking that the purpose of a college education is to land a well-paying job. Yet, millions of people with a college education don't enjoy their jobs and career choices, aren't paid well, and aren't sure what else they could do with their lives. Furthermore, some who may enjoy their jobs feel limited -- and are limited -- with the narrowness of their education. You must have heard people say, "I can't write well, I am an accountant," or "I am not a business person, I don't know how to invest," or "I know nothing about politics, since I studied math," and so on.

As human beings, we are meant to recognize our fundamental goodness, pursue our greatest aspirations, achieve fulfillment, and live lives we have imagined. Formal education can either be extremely helpful or incredibly limiting in this endeavor. It comes down to our understanding of education -- its purpose and potential -- and what we do with it. College education can either transform your life, strengthen your character, help you identify who you are and what you stand for, and set you on a path to happiness -- or, it can be a waste of time, effort, and money. As always, the choice is yours.

It took me a long time to understand what going to college really meant for me and why I fell so deeply in love with St. Norbert. I completed my degree with two majors and a minor, graduating in four years and without debt. Yet, it was the other stuff that made my experience so rewarding. My time at St. Norbert was not easy. I struggled to pay my bills during my entire time there. I worked a lot; one particular semester, I held two internships, co-taught a class, ran a college newspaper, worked to resurrect the yearbook and host a journalism conference, founded one student organization and presided over another, and served at several committees -- while taking four classes and searching for a post-graduation job. Needless to say, it was busy, it was challenging, it was exciting, and above all, it was rewarding.

And here's why.

I love learning, but most of what I learned in classroom I could have learned on my own. What I could not have done, however, was explore life, experience the world, and test my ideas in a fairly safe and confined environment, with a few major, life-long repercussions. Yes, a vice president at St. Norbert once threatened to kick me out because I challenged the system too much; I was betrayed by some "friends;" and I dealt with a couple of incredibly arrogant faculty members throughout my time there. At the same time, I was able to explore my identity, discover my passions, work for truth and justice, and learn more about life, the world, and myself. I formed relationships that are still strong, experienced events that transformed me, and ultimately found a place and people who accepted me, flaws and all, and challenged and encouraged me to change myself, change my community, and change the world for the better.

Not all colleges do this, of course, but the good ones often do. However, their ability to do so has to do with our attitude. If we are there simply to get a diploma that would lead to a job, they can do little for us. On the other hand, if we are there for a "rite of passage," a journey to transform us from children into adults, able of leaving our mark on this world – then we're in the right place.

One of my favorite lessons from a college professor is that the best answer to every question is: it depends. So, when contemplating if college education is worth it, the answer is: it depends. *What do you hope to accomplish? What does formal education mean to you? How will you use it? Why are you doing it? Why not? Why would you recommend it to others? Do you regret spending money on it?* Answers to these and other questions are personal and they are completely your own. As you contemplate them, either through a reflection of your past, or consideration for the future, take a moment to assess the following:

1. Knowledge is power, which has the capacity to solve some of the greatest ills of our human race, both individual and collective. Learning is *always* a worthwhile pursuit.

2. Formal education offers a place for learning without limits, in a safe, structured, and generally disciplined space. In fact, it often serves as a way to encourage us to learn more.

3. True learning in a formal setting, be it high school, college or graduate school, is only possible if we throw away the idea that education is a means to an end rather than an end itself.

4. Specialized degrees, such as law, medicine, dentistry, design, etc. are tools that help us live out our purpose. Our degrees, titles, and the validation they give us do not define who we are nor do they define our purpose.

5. Learning goes beyond the skills-based education. Learning includes discovering who we are, what we believe in, what the world is like, what we want our future to be, what makes us tick, and so on.

Formal education is not for everyone, but I believe it is a good idea for most people. If you want to live a good life then consider what an education can offer you and pursue it with passion. Make it your own. Put demands on your college to offer you the best possible education. When I was at St. Norbert, I challenged the system, because I believed that the college could do a better job in transforming its students. It already did well, but I demanded more. Fill in the blank for the college you are choosing: "If I am going to pay $40,000 to go here, this college better... (fill in the blank)."

By taking responsibility and owning your formal education, you will make the most out of it and later on consider it worthy of every last cent.

14. GETTING INTO A SCHOOL
OF YOUR CHOICE

Cauliflower is nothing else but cabbage with a
college education.
MARK TWAIN

When I was a little boy, I dreamed of attending Harvard University after watching a movie where one of the characters, a graduate of Harvard Law, was making $500/hr. I don't remember the name of the movie nor the storyline, but I can vividly recall spending hours daydreaming about the day when I, too, would be a successful, rich Harvard grad. In the years that followed, however, I lost sight of this dream in large part because getting into Harvard proved to be a lot more difficult than I originally thought. I also found myself scrambling to pay for an education -- any education -- so being picky was not an option. So I decided to dream in a different direction.

Ironically, it was within the first few months of my college career that I heard someone refer to St. Norbert College as "Harvard of the Midwest." I chuckled, because a part of me knew that I landed where I was meant to be. Don't get me wrong, St. Norbert is not Harvard, but my experience there proved that life works in mysterious ways and that sometimes it is okay if our childhood dreams don't come true, because they leave space for new experiences to organically develop. During this process, I also learned several lessons about "colleges of choice," how to pick the right one, how to avoid picking the wrong one, and how to get into a college. Any college.

I did not get into Harvard, but I cannot imagine how different my life would have been if I did. When I think of all the experiences I have had thus far, the people that I have met and the lessons I have learned, I never once regret that I did not work harder to get in. Nor do I ever think that somehow I missed out because of it.

College is what you make of it. It does not matter if it is Harvard or St. Norbert or some third place. Each place has its pluses and minuses, and each place can offer a transformative experience. Sure, the world may rank one higher than the other, but in essence, learning and opportunities to learn don't change. And each place *will* transform you in some way; how far and how much is up to you.

With that out of the way, here are several concrete steps on how to get into a school of your choice that I learned through my failures:

1. Apply: One of the most common obstacles to people's ability to achieve anything is their failure at giving it a shot. I never applied to Harvard College, so no wonder I never got in.

2. Understand the culture: Read and learn everything you can about the school or schools of your choice. Don't just focus on the fancy information (e.g. how prestigious they are); rather, try to understand the culture. Try to meet with people who went there and see if you like their personalities. Each place has their own spirit, their ethos, and you should find out what it is before you waste your time trying to get in. Another good way of gauging the culture is by visiting the campus and talking to average students and faculty. For example, after your traditional admissions tour is done, walk over to the student center or the cafeteria and people-watch. Talk to regular students and watch their body language when they tell you about the school; if you pay attention to what they are really saying, you will know how much they *really* like it -- or don't like it.

3. Understand the requirements: If a college tells you that they are looking at a whole person, but still require you to submit standardized tests (this is especially true with graduate schools) and assert that most of the applicants do "very well" on them, be aware that what they are really saying is: standardized tests are critical. Similarly, pay attention to recommendation requirements -- and be careful who you choose to ask to write you one -- and your essay. Try to read between the lines. Call an admission officer and ask questions. Lot of questions.

4. Standardized Tests: I find ACT, SAT, GRE, GMAT, and other standardized tests painful and useless, because I do not believe they give an accurate picture of one's intellect or their ability to succeed. Rather, I think, they place people into a box and only a certain kind of student does well. They often miss the true potential that a student has, especially when attempting to go to college. It is ironic because as colleges and universities tout their commitment to diversity of backgrounds and ideas, they embrace tests that "standardize" people. That's so foolish. We all have different educational backgrounds, because we have been taught by different teachers, raised by different people, grew up in unique environments, and informed our existence through specific experiences. Trying to put our intellect, our potential, and our capacity for success into a box is ridiculous.

This is all subjective, of course. Therefore, if you want to get into a school of your choice, make sure you *ace* the required standardized tests. Spend the necessary time and effort studying and understand the best strategy of conquering them. It has less to do with intelligence and more to do with the rules... at least the tests that I have taken. Thus, learn the rules, ask for help, and prepare vigorously. Do *not* diminish the role these tests play in your admission even if you think you have an amazing story to tell. (I did too, but the Stanford Business School thought otherwise!)

5. Recommendations: These are really important in your application process, but only if they come from the appropriate sources and contain the right language. Make sure your recommendations are diverse, very specific with examples that back up the statements, and have them come from people who have accomplished much or have a connection to the school of your choice. For example, if you know a local judge or a well-known businessman, their word for your capacity to succeed is much stronger than that of a teacher. Not because a teacher knows less –a teacher may know you better and be more credible, but in the eyes of an admission counselor, a teacher that you choose to write a recommendation will rave about you regardless of it being true or not. Besides, they write dozens, sometime hundreds of them, annually. At the same time, a local executive, a wealthy community volunteer, or a top athlete are likely to write only a few and -- the perception goes -- only if you are worthy. Find someone whose voice will help you. Similarly, you can look for an alumnus or alumna of the school you are applying to; the idea is that because they went to the said college, they would know if you would do well or not.

If you cannot find anyone "famous" to write you a recommendation, ask the people -- teachers, coaches, employers -- that you trust and give them some suggestions on what you would like them to include. Most people would rather have guidance then shoot in the dark, or be generic. The last thing you want them to do is be generic. If you need three recommendations, for example, give each of the people writing them, slightly different suggestions, because the idea is that between all three of them they will paint a well-rounded picture of you and make a stronger case for you.

6. *Tell the truth:* With great recommendations in your hand and top scores on the standardized tests, its time to write your own essays. Tell your story, truthfully and simply. Do not follow the "what they want to hear logic" but be honest. Admissions committees read *a lot* of applications. Find a way to make yours stick out. The only caveat to this is that the application needs to fall within the framework of a student they are looking for and the culture they maintain. That is to say, you may have a great essay and really be memorable, but not be the right fit for the school. This is where some people would advise you to understand what they want and tailor your story to fit within this expectation. I would advise you otherwise, because if they don't want your authentic story, your aspirations, your way of thinking, and your approach, that means they don't want you. Why would you want to go there?

One of the reasons I fell in love with St. Norbert was because this was the place that wanted me. A lot of schools said no. St. Norbert not only said yes, they also put in the work to help me get there. That's huge and something I won't ever forget. Given the unique role colleges can play in your personal development, the relationship you ought to form with your school is for a lifetime. If they aren't willing to take you -- just the way you are -- there's no point going there. Look elsewhere. There are thousands of colleges and universities in the United States. Don't settle.

7. *Trust but Verify:* I believe that if you follow these tips closely, you have a very good chance of getting in the school of your choice. Then again, even if you are among the best possible applicants, top schools don't have enough spots and it can be nuances that decide between you and another person. Don't sweat, however. There is always another year to re-apply. Another year of experiences may make you even more appealing.

Do not give up. Try at least two or three times. At the same time, make sure you apply to other places too ... even if they are back ups. A friend recently applied only to the University of Chicago public policy master's program. He had a great shot, but he got wait-listed. Yet, no matter how many times I told him to apply elsewhere, he wouldn't listen. As you can guess, by the time August rolled around, he regretted this decision. Have a back up plan!

Finally, applying to colleges and graduate school is sometimes a chance of luck. In the end, no matter how hard you try, you will attend the school you are meant to. And, in the big scheme of things, that is okay. I will tell you a secret: when I was looking into grad schools, I badly wanted to attend Stanford Business School. I did not get in. I was upset. I thought this happened because I wasn't good enough. Had I studied harder for my GRE (I studied only for about six or seven hours) or written a better application, I thought I would have been in. The narrative of self-doubt and putting myself down plagued me for a while. At one point, however, I realized: it was a good thing I did not get into Stanford because, otherwise, I would not have attended Loyola University Chicago. More importantly, if I had gone to Stanford, I would not have met the people that I have, who have changed and enriched my life, nor would have I be writing this book.

Life works in mysterious ways, but the only thing that is constant in life is change. Accordingly, while you should always pursue your dreams fervently, focus on your purpose instead of specific ways of getting somewhere -- and let the universe do its part in getting you there in a way that is most beneficial to you, even if you don't see it at the time.

All you can do is give it your all and trust that the best is to come..

15. WHEN CLASS PERFORMANCE AND GRADES MATTER

> *There are advantages to being elected President. The day after I was elected, I had my high school grades classified Top Secret.*
> RONALD REAGAN

If you love learning, or you don't, that is up to you. However, the hard truth is that to get into a reputable college or graduate school, and especially to win scholarships, grades matter. It is quite simple.

In the old days, people understood well the importance of learning and those who were able to afford such commodities would send their children off to expensive boarding schools or home-school them and bring in top teachers. Thankfully, times have changed drastically for many of us in the Western world, and access to education has become easier than ever. Not only has it become a norm for people to get educated, but attaining a college degree has also become a part of the proverbial America Dream.

Easier as it may be, it is still difficult, and it still depends on good grades. But good grades and overall academic success are not won only by acing exams. They are won by your passions; your relationships with instructors and your peers; your desire to learn and excel; and, ultimately, your willingness to work hard. They are also won by your *overall* performance in all classes, not a single class.

With that said, there is a logic to this madness of successful academic career, but it begins, like anything else in life, with your choice, your resoluteness to do well. Whatever your motivation, make sure to have one. Not the one that is imposed on you, but the one that is burning within you and use that motivation to push ahead.

And then, use some of these tips to perform well:

1. Get to know your teacher. It's never about projects; it's always about relationships. If your teacher knows more about you than your name, they will be more inclined to help you do well. Give you more attention. Guide you. Support you. Of course, you have to do your part by being respectful, fair, and hard working, but don't disregard the importance of engaging your professor. In addition to their academic help, you just might land a mentor and perhaps a friend for life. And those two things are priceless.

Note: if there is one thing that you can take away from this book let that be the fundamental respect for all human beings. You can dislike (and you will dislike) people, disagree with them, and not enjoy their company. But you must respect them. Because, if you can't respect others, how can others respect you?

Now, this translates into classroom, too. You can be "buddy-buddy" with a teacher and your peers, but if you don't respect their deadlines and don't do your work, your relationships *will* suffer. In fact, your closeness to the teacher will seem phony and self-serving, instead of a genuine quest for connection. And your relationship with your peers will suffer because you won't be viewed as trustworthy or reliable.

2. Be open and leave ego at the door. If you don't understand something, the only way you can understand it is by asking a question. And then another question. Then a dozen more if you need to, and from more than a dozen different people, until you find the answer. Doing well sometimes means removing your preconceived notions about the class (e.g. that teacher sucks, their class is boring, etc.)

There are teachers who are boring and should never be teaching and there are classes that I wish I never took. But often, we waste more energy complaining instead of getting things done. And sometimes, we walk into a classroom with preconceived notions, and instead of finding something interesting about the class, we dread it. Do the opposite: do not judge it, but find something interesting and get it done (even if you have to cross days on your calendar before the experience is over. I've done that.).

3. Sometimes, you just need to do enough to get by. Some of us are simply not wired to grasp certain topics, and that is okay. I have done this myself and have seen many others beat themselves up over sucking at one particular class. In fact, I have seen this so often in college where students spend 80% of time on one class -- the one they dread and are doing poorly in -- and 20% on the rest of them. The outcome is pretty clear: they get burnt out, other classes suffer, they don't enjoy any of the classes as much as they would have, and ultimately they still don't do well in the "tough" class.

Some of this approach is cultural, but some of it is purely counterintuitive. Why would you waste 80% of your life on something you loath. If the class is not required, drop it and take something more interesting. If the class is required, than suck it up and do enough to get by. On the other hand, put the extra energy at doing great in the other classes.

Much of our approach in education, psychology, and personal development until recently has been focused on discovering the problem areas and addressing those. In my experience, that's not always helpful. Do the best you can in any given moment, but don't feel bad for not being great in every area (or think that you can't be good in any area just because you have done poorly in some). That simply isn't possible. Instead, focus on discovering all the areas that you are good at and do well.

4. To that last point, figure out what you are good at and what your passions are as early as you can and follow them vigorously. Be honest about yourself and don't worry about people telling you that you "need" or that you "should" take certain classes. Or that a particular field isn't good enough.

As I said earlier, my dad is an engineer with a great love for technology and computer programming, so when I found my passions in history and political science, he grumbled. Even my sister told me once that without a "Calculus" class, I wouldn't get into college. Well, I knew that if I had taken that calc class, I would have ended up with a D. So, I dropped it and took Psychology. I got an A. And I have done well with my Political Science degrees.

Follow your own passions. Studying psychology, for example, doesn't mean you will become a psychologist. But it might mean that you will love what you are studying, you will do well at it (and make sure you do get A's) and that enthusiasm will allow you to achieve great things in life.

5. Final point for this chapter: if you are struggling with your ability to learn and believe you may have a medical condition (e.g. dyslexia, ADHD, etc.), do not be ashamed to seek help. If people don't believe you at first, have the courage to find those who will. Having dyslexia and being aware of it, for example, can help you go even further in life, but it will only harm you if you do not acknowledge that you have different learning needs. There's absolutely no shame in that. There's only shame when we as a society do not provide enough opportunities for those with learning disabilities. Make sure to speak up!

16. WHEN CLASSROOM ISN'T ENOUGH

Study: the act of texting, eating, and watching TV with an open book nearby.
UNKNOWN

I wrote a lot about community service in an earlier chapter about serving the world, however, I felt it was important to bring it up again, specifically in the context of formal educational pursuits.

It is true that grades matter. But it is even more true that classroom performance is not enough to take you where you need and want to go. In my own experience, it was involvement in high school that help me get into college; it was my college involvement that demonstrated my true capacity and introduced me to the people who in turn gave me many career opportunities. And most of the friendships I acquired also happened through my involvement. Thus, I strongly encourage you to follow your passions in getting involved and allowing yourself to drop your textbooks, from time to time, in exchange for social experiences, which will not only enrich your life and last a lifetime, but they will also help advance your development and your career in a meaningful way.

Student Organizations

Get involved in students organizations that are available at your school. Yes, sometimes you would rather spend time watching movies or just chilling at your residence hall, but getting out of your comfort zone, meeting new people, and volunteering will make your life better.

Getting involved with student groups will offer you a structured way to meet people, it will give you meaning through membership -- and also a reason to get up out of the bed sometimes -- and it will teach you how to organize programs, execute projects, work with people, work in teams, learn your leadership style, and lead meetings. All of these skills are transferrable and will benefit you later in your life (provided you actually learn them instead of pretending that you know them).

Involvement in student groups will also teach you personal responsibility and commitment that derives from your own decisions, not out of the feelings of guilt or requirement. You have to go to class if you want to finish college, but you don't have to be involved in student groups. Which is why, if you do get involved, that involvement will teach you stuff and test (and strengthen) your character and work ethic.

One Time Service Projects

Sometimes, you may not have the time to be involved with every organization, but that doesn't mean you cannot help out on a one-time basis. Many colleges offer those opportunities, and usually in the beginning of the Fall semester or later in Spring. Two such major initiatives that come to mind are Make a Difference Day and Global Youth Service Day.

Many schools also observe the Dr. Martin Luther King, Jr. Day through service. These events can often lead to much greater opportunities down the road, too.

For example, my freshman year in college, I volunteered at

the Peace and Justice Center, making wooden crosses -- 2,000 of them -- to commemorate the 2,000 U.S. soldiers that had died in Iraq War by that point. Through this experience, I met the director of the center, who would only a few months later offer me an internship and would step in to offer help with my financial struggles later on. I never forgot that, or how a seemingly innocent encounter led to a relationship.

Internships
I held six internships during my college career.
Why?
Because they are awesome. Generally, internships are designed to help you learn particular skills or lessons, they allow you to take responsibility and take risks, with few consequences if any, and in many instances, they are paid. But even when they are not, they give you an opportunity to experience what it is like to work on projects that are often very different and for very different organizations.

For example, I spent nearly two years interning at an award-winning marketing and advertising agency called Arketype where I had a unique opportunity to work on the region's branding initiative, help produce a music compilation and contribute in other areas. More importantly, I also formed meaningful friendships.

On the other hand, during that same time, I also held an internship with a local Chamber of Commerce. Another great experience, but very different both in terms of projects and also the organizational culture. In both instances, I learned a lot and often the kind of knowledge that is transferrable and that I was able to use elsewhere.

Having such interesting and different internships made me a lot more well-rounded; it allowed me to interact and build relationships with different groups of people; and, it taught me about different styles of leadership, different types of work, and different types of organizational culture -- all of which helped me better understand my own working preferences.

Another great thing about internships is that they are usually time-constrained to several months or a year. This gives student a chance to experience something, learn something, but then move on. Of course, some internships can last longer and often turn into full-time jobs. I should also mention that if you are concerned that your internship won't be paid, still take it. For example, my Chamber internship was unpaid and was created only after I reached out to them and asked if I could help.

Social Life
One of the few regrets that I have is not spending more time with friends while I was in college; cooking dinner, hanging out, playing charades, going out and just socializing. Most of my socializing was structured and unless it had a specific purpose or was done with people who were the closest to me, it rarely happened spontaneously. I was so focused on "succeeding" and advancing myself that I had to always be doing something.

I couldn't just be.

I can count how many times I went out with people or spent a weekend just wasting my time watching TV or playing cards. My freshman year I did more of this, but once the bug of involvement bit me, I was off and going.

This approach pushed me out of balance and it also isolated me from many people who viewed me as unapproachable. Thankfully, I was able to form some friendships, but I wish I did more of that, and here's why: it's college.

A big part of using your college experience as the rite of passage is to meet different people, get to know them, share your vulnerabilities, experiment, get into arguments, make plans to change the world, laugh to tears, and share secrets. If you don't do these things in college -- if you don't explore, experience, and express your genuine self -- I promise that it will catch up with you later. Maybe in your 20s, as it happened with me, or in your 30s or even later.

One of the best pieces of advice I received in college was from the former Dean of Students who told me: "Give yourself a hug. Just do it. You have to." And he was right. I didn't do it then, but I have since. The best advice I received in graduate school from professors was: "Don't be stupid." At first I was confused, but then it made sense.

Use your time in college or graduate school to explore life. Yes, be fully focused and disciplined to achieve your academic, career, and extra-curricular goals. But don't forget to give yourself a hug if you don't get all As or if things don't pan out exactly as you want them.

Similarly, don't be too scared to put yourself out there and meet new people and explore life. Go out, have a drink, be vulnerable, have fun and take risks. Just don't be stupid.

We have all been in situations when we did some things that we shouldn't have and aren't proud of. Maybe we partied too hard, or got into a fight, or even considered sitting behind the wheel while drunk. Maybe we drank underage. The thing is: if you did it, and got away with it, don't be stupid and do it again. If you didn't do it, don't be stupid and do it to begin with. There's a way to enjoy life, have fun, explore, meet people, party and make the most out of your every experience, but that does not have to mean you have to be stupid to put your life and the life of others at risk.

Life can be hard as is, don't make it harder. Be smart. Be positive. And have fun!

ADI REDZIC

17. PAYING FOR
   YOUR EDUCATION

> *Schools and the means of education shall forever
> be encouraged.*
> NORTHWEST ORDINANCE,
> CONTINENTAL CONGRESS, 1878

When I came to the United States in 2004, I was 17 years old with $375 in my pockets, two suitcases and a dream. This dream was to get an American education, but all odds were against me.

Not only was I broke, homesick, and struggling with my identity and loneliness, but I was experiencing all this in another country and in another language. I was also not eligible to work, seek federal financial aid (loans, grants, etc.) or win most college scholarships offered to traditional American students. In fact, most universities at that time had little to no money dedicated for international students, and those that did offer some dollars rarely covered more than 1/3 of tuition.

For example, top scholarship for an international student at St. Norbert in 2005 was $8,500/year. Top scholarship for an American student was roughly $25,000/year. Thankfully, this gap has been bridged since.

Additionally, I had no stable sources of income and my

parents weren't able to support me much either; the average salary in Montenegro at that time was a little bit over $50 a month. My options were limited, but also simple: give up on my dream and return to Montenegro or find a way against all odds.

Thankfully, I found a way.

This process was neither easy nor was it simple -- and most of the time, I had no idea what I was doing -- but I knew one thing: failure was not an option. It will surprise you how creative you can get when the walls are closing on you and your options keep disappearing. If someone would ask me today to explain how I did it in one word, I would say: tenacity. In fact, that was the word that the head of admissions at St. Norbert used to describe me back in 2005. *Tenacity* is essential for anything in life. So, if you are wondering how you, too, can pay for your education, tenacity is the answer.

Beyond trying so many schools, once I got into college, I held six internships and a couple of other on-campus jobs as a way of supporting myself and paying college bills. I networked with a lot of people and often told my story, shamelessly. I asked for help in the form of personal fundraising in order to bridge the gap; I stuck to a very strict budget and applied for a lot of small scholarships, most of which I never won; however, I didn't need many, just a few. I also became very friendly with the college's Bursar who did her best to help by being flexible in offering a very specific payment plan that worked for me and by trusting that I would pay. Too many times, I received a notification of a hold on my account due to an overdue bill, which precluded me from registering for the following semester. Those experiences were traumatic, but thanks to my ongoing relationship with the Bursar and consistent search for and caution with money -- throughout all four years of my college education -- as well as my track record and perhaps persuasion, somehow we always resolved it.

Hindsight is 20:20 vision, and it is only now in retrospect

that I can see how valuable that struggle was: It made me resilient in the face of obstacles; it taught me to be comfortable with, or at least manage, uncertainty; it inspired me to dream and never hesitate to pursue those dreams out of fear that they might not come true or because others think that they wouldn't. And it reaffirmed that the only time we really, truly fail is the time we give up. I also graduated with no debt.

Although you may be thinking it, make no mistake: you and I are not that different. Our circumstances may be different, but our potential for success is not. In trying to give answers on how you can pay for your education, it is impossible to predict every imaginable scenario and every unique situation. However, what I can do is offer main pointers that you can apply in your own quest to fund your education.

Financial Aid Overview
When attending college in the United States, and if you are a citizen or permanent resident, student financial aid is a four-legged stool: it consists of scholarships (free money, usually merit-based with varying requirements), grants (free money, usually need-based), student loans (not free money, need to be repaid), and work-study dollars (opportunity to hold an on-campus job and earn money through federal subsidy).

The first three are further broken down into sub-categories based on the source, type, and purpose.

For example, most colleges have some form of merit-based scholarships. Many schools also have specific scholarships for specific students; for instance, transfer scholarships, international scholarships, diversity scholarships, first-generation college student scholarships, and departmental scholarships (e.g. if you want to study music, you may be awarded a music scholarship).

Universities also have grants that they give out.

Similarly, both state and federal governments have grants they award, and some states and the federal government have loans as well.

When you apply to college, generally, the college's Financial Aid office will come back to you with a "Financial Aid Package" offer, which includes one or more of these options. Of course, there are also instances where no financial aid dollars are offered due to one's ineligibility. For example, some schools still do not offer any dollars to international students. In terms of university scholarships and grants, if your grades aren't good enough, you may not be rewarded anything -- or a lot less than your peers with better grades, hence the expression "merit-based" scholarships. Or, perhaps your family has substantial resources as indicated on their tax returns, and they claim you as a dependent, therefore you may not qualify for financial aid. But how would they know that, you wonder?

The answer is: FAFSA.

When you apply to college, if you are a citizen or permanent resident, you will fill out FAFSA: Free Application for Federal Student Aid, which is a form used to apply for financial aid from the U.S. Department of Education and is also used to apply for state grants and aid from colleges and universities. FAFSA collects financial information about the student (and their parents if they are a dependent and/or their spouse if they are married) and calculates EFC: Expected Family Contribution--the amount they believe the student and/or their family would be able to contribute towards college expenses. The remaining amount is covered through a combination of institutional scholarships and grants, federal and state grants, and federal student loans.

FAFSA is what allows university's Financial Aid offices to put together a "Financial Aid Package."

Even if your family is blessed with wealth, you can still take advantage of the federal aid programs and you may be surprised at how much money you will be rewarded regardless of your financial circumstances. Of course, you want to try to take university or federal aid (scholarships and grants), but not loans since they need to be repaid with interest. In case you do need to take on loans, it is still a better deal, because the federal government offers lower rates than most private lenders. You can file and learn everything about FAFSA on the U.S. Department of Education website.

Finally, there are also many outside scholarships offered by corporations, private foundations, and wealthy individuals. If your parent works at a university, you may be eligible to receive tuition benefits (i.e. free tuition) at that school or through tuition exchange with another university.

Sometimes, larger corporations also have programs to assist children of their employees with college expenses or, if you already have a full-time job, talk to your employer, maybe they will help pay for your education. Many do.

You also may find financial help in form of scholarships, grants, and donations at your local church, synagogue, masque, or temple. And, at those special and most fortunate of occasions -- which happen more often than you know -- there may be wealthy individuals who will personally help you out.

In any event: funding is there, you just need to find it.

Student Loans

There are two different student loan programs in the United States at the moment. They are Direct Loan Program where the lender is the U.S. Department of Education. There are three types of these loans:

Direct Subsidized Loans, which are made to eligible students who demonstrate financial need. They have better loan terms to help undergraduate students with actual financial need.

Direct Unsubsidized Loans, which are made to undergraduate and graduate students, but students are not required to demonstrate financial need.

Direct PLUS Loans, which are made to graduate

students and parents to cover school expenses not covered by subsidized or unsubsidized loans. The interest rates on these loans are the highest of all federal student loans.

The other student loan program is *Federal Perkins Loan Program*, where the lender is the school for undergraduate and graduate students with exceptional financial need.

Finally, there are also **non-government loans**, which are extended to students by private financial institutions and are based on their credit-worthiness and usually require co-signers. These generally have rather high interest rates.

The difference between all these loans is the eligibility to receive them, the interest rates, and the source. In all of these cases, getting a loan means you need to pay it back with interest. In most cases, however, you do not have to pay anything until you are done with your education. Typically, you must begin to repay your loans six months after graduation, however you want to make sure you are clear on those terms before you take out loan(s) in the first place.

In an ideal situation, you would not take out any loans, but if you have to, I would strongly advise you to consider what amount you actually need as opposed to the amount you want and to explore -- and exhaust -- other funding options before you take up these loans. A good rule of thumb is: do not use student loans to cover more than 5-10% of your educational expenses, unless you absolutely have to. If you do, however, find yourself with loans after graduation, keep in mind that you may apply for deferment or forbearance of your loan if you meet certain criteria. Deferment or forbearance allow you to delay payment or reduce it. However, you need to carefully explore those options because not everyone qualifies.

Scholarships and Grants
Most universities offer institutional scholarships based on merit and students are usually automatically considered for

these. Most places don't offer full-ride or even full-tuition scholarships, but some do. Places like Harvard or Princeton offer need-blind based admission, which means that if you get in, they will find a way for you to attend regardless of your financial need. Other places do look at your ability to pay as a basis of admission.

Beyond automatic scholarships, there are those that come from specific sources or particular departments and they may require a separate application/essay or even an audition or an interview to select recipients. Those are obviously harder to get, but they are worth the effort. If you do go after those -- in this day and age of internet -- do your homework in figuring out who you would be meeting with. Maybe you can find a common touch with them, a person you both know, or better understand how to connect with them. Even though scholarships are "merit-based" and there is indeed a certain degree of meritocracy, we are all still human. We resonate and like certain people more than others.

When applying for scholarships -- just like with jobs -- make sure you understand your audience. Consider who established or funds the scholarship, what they are like, that the spirit of scholarship is, and what they are looking for. Sometimes, you won't match well with them. Other times, however, it is purely a matter of emphasizing one side of you so that they can better understand how you are the right choice for said scholarship.

Remember, scholarship reviewers usually receive many applications, so it is up to you to connect the dots for them so that they notice you and ultimately pick you for the award. That said: make sure you are always honest and as true to yourself as possible. It is because of their experience that they can notice when someone is trying too hard to impress them. That's a turn off.

It is also really important that you research university websites for all potential sources of aid: institutional scholarships; departmental scholarships; scholarships given by a particular office on campus; scholarships that you may qualify for later on in your college career; or, even looking at scholarships that at first glance you are not eligible for, but the eligibility may be stretched in some way (e.g. a diversity scholarship intended for racial diversity may also be extended to a Caucasian international student).

When you are equipped with all this knowledge and have a big picture, it is much easier to understand your options and ask additional questions.

Do not rely completely on financial aid and admission officers in understanding what scholarships are available. As much as most of them would like to help you, and some really do, admission recruiters are often sales people trying to get you to come to college and they want to make sure that you can pay. Rarely will you find people who will get creative and go out of their own way to help you attend their school by calling in favors and finding some money, somewhere. Sometimes, they simply don't have all the information in part because in many instances they don't decide on certain funding sources or they don't have access to it.

For example, when I first applied to St. Norbert, the Dean of Admission who was in place then did not necessarily see the value in having me attend, so he used a basic formula in accepting me: since my grades from back home were transfers (thus he did not see the As, just "transfer") and I did not do very well on the ACT, I was awarded $7,500/year scholarship (even though the highest was $8,500). I did have almost all As, but he was not impressed with my work with UNICEF or my background. As I learned later on, he was also busy looking for another job.

Thankfully, when I called again at the end of July, the new head of admission had the opposite perspective. She saw something in me and thought that I should definitely come to St. Norbert. She also awarded me the top scholarship and she then contacted the Norbertine Fathers to ask them to support my education. She also gave me a job to work for her, and then suggested that I apply for a Resident Assistant position for the other three years of my college career as a way of covering room and board.

In addition to it being a mysterious way of life, this story is also an example of how important it is that you communicate your story time and again and keep in mind that we are all human: two people in the same position may have completely different priorities and view you completely differently.

So, if they say "no" at first, you try again.

In addition to entrance scholarships, most colleges have scholarships or awards that you can win throughout your time there.

For example, my sophomore year, I won the Hanke Peace and Justice scholarship by applying for it. When you research scholarships, take note of those that might be available to you later on and put it in your calendar. You may not win them all, but you can at least try. Another thing about colleges and named scholarships is that you may be awarded a new scholarship or the amount may increase because a donor decided to give more money to the college and support students.

The scholarship opportunities are there, just keep looking for them. That said, there aren't enough scholarships at most colleges to cover everyone, so you have to look elsewhere.

Thankfully, in addition to institutional scholarships, there are many outside scholarships, too. In fact, there are so many scholarships -- and so few qualified applicants who actually apply -- that there is money left on the table every year. When I was searching for money, I found a website that had tons of scholarship opportunities and I kept applying, even when I was not eligible due to my "international student" status (I was hoping they would make an exception). However, if this is not an obstacle for you, look at outside scholarships and APPLY.

The reason why many scholarships aren't awarded is because many qualified young people do not have the courage to apply, believing that they wouldn't get it anyway. So, they wonder: *what's the point?*

The point is that you miss 100% of the shots that you do

not take. You don't know that you won't get it until you apply, but if you don't apply, you are definitely not getting it. There are so many scholarships out there that odds are in your favor.

For example, you can use www.fastweb.com to look for them. Or even search for scholarships through your local Chamber of Commerce or other local organizations and community foundations. For example, in Green Bay, there's an organization called Scholarships Inc. that gives out scholarships to students from the area or who are attending area schools. Many times, major corporations or individuals in the community will have scholarships too.

Many wealthy individuals and corporations create foundations and fund scholarships for students who promise potential or come from particular backgrounds. Sometimes they do it to honor someone, certain values, or in their own name. Most of the scholarships that you can apply for are created this way. While you can certainly see someone's name on the building and try to meet them or write to them, tell them your story, and ask them for help, you can also do another thing: use the wisdom from fundraising when applying for scholarships. There are three main components to fundraising: ability to give, linkage (that is to say, how they are connected to you and how you are connected to them), and affinity to give -- in this case, give to you. In other words, try to make a connection.

When you apply for scholarships, don't just look at the obvious qualifications, but see where they are coming from, who established the scholarship, what their background is, and if your background matches theirs. If you have an opportunity, ask people who have been around longer to give you some insights.

When you write your application, do not think of the person reading it but the person who established it (unless it's the same person). The person reading it will award the scholarship to the one that most speaks to the spirit of the scholarship's creator. This is, again, relationship building. You may not have the benefit to meet people who might help fund your education, but do not view scholarship or grant applications as a form, but view it as relationship even if you have to imagine what that relationship would be like. Understand why they would give in the first place, and why they would give to you in particular, and match your experience and your talents with that. Don't think of what they would like to hear, and say that -- they will read through that right away -- but tell them your story as genuinely as you can, within the context of what they are looking for, and things will happen.

In addition to being international and ineligible for most scholarships, another reason why I struggled so much to find funding was because I had no idea how many opportunities were available.

Recently, I heard a story of a young woman in her senior year of college who was short a thousand dollars after all financial aid and anticipated work income was exhausted, so she was contemplating quitting her schooling. I was baffled (this was also when I decided to definitely write this book). Finding a thousand dollars in Montenegro, especially to fund your education, would be fairly difficult even today. However, finding a thousand dollars in the United States for such a worthy cause is not that difficult.

If you are still reading this book and are determined to go to college, or go back to school, you definitely have what it takes to find and win scholarships. Just go forward and ask, apply, and remain persistent. The money will come.

As with scholarships, so with grants, except grants are more specific and they are need-based. (In other words, you have to demonstrate that you have a financial need.) Scholarships don't have to be, grants usually are. So, search for grants both internally and externally that you might qualify for and apply. Grants, like scholarships, don't have to be local or statewide either. Look everywhere and tell your story, be authentic, write in a compelling way, and you are likely to get something.

Work

There are many inspiring stories of people who put themselves through college by working a couple of jobs while attending school full-time. If you have that option -- and many do -- it is worth exploring.

What do you want from your college experience? What others options do you have? Can you get some financial aid in the form of grants and scholarships (both of which you don't have to pay back) and then cover the rest of your expenses through work?

All four years of my college journey, I spent my summers working 40 hours a week and during the school year I worked 20 hours a week, which was my limit as an international student. I worked all kinds of jobs: from campus security, where I was dealing with drunken people, unlocking doors, and cleaning puke – to working at an advertising firm. I was willing to do anything short of prostitution or something illegal or unethical. Honest work, and there I was. And at one occasion when I was laid off due to funding constraints, I quickly found two other jobs: one 5-7 hours and another 12-15 hours a week in order to meet my 20-hour maximum and earn as much as I could.

I worked minimum wage jobs and sometimes convinced people to hire me for positions they didn't even have or find money in other areas of their budget and re-allocate it. When it comes to budgetary and other constraints, for the first two and a half years of my college education, my jobs had to be on campus, which posed a problem if department had no money to pay me. Unlike work-study, which is funded with the help from the federal government, which I was not eligible for, my jobs came directly from the departmental budgets. And, sadly, when universities cut budgets, student employment hours tend to be cut first.

Although I had a great time working campus jobs, if you have that option, look outside of the campus, too, because they may pay more. You can also do some side projects that can get you some spending money in addition to your standard job or internship. *What about working a lot of hours during the summer and winter breaks? What about doing freelance work on the weekends or picking up a couple of shifts at a bar or coffee shop from time to time?*

Another option would be to look for college positions that may give you a stipend, but then they also cover your meals and lodging. For example, the coveted resident assistant positions are great because they give you a room, a meal plan, and you get a stipend. Sometimes, you are even allowed to work on campus for another five hours a week or so.

Also, teaching assistantships may offer some benefits, though more so in graduate school. Although this chapter is useful in both undergraduate and graduate pursuits, if you are going to get a Ph.D., do not pay for it out of pocket. Most universities offer assistantships to Ph.D. candidates. And if they don't, find another school.

Sometimes, schools also have "faculty-student research partnerships" where they award incoming students with a grant to work with a faculty or staff member on a project or conduct research. Ask about those. Students are not always automatically considered for those and sometimes the money for them comes from a grant a faculty has received and it is up to the faculty to make hiring decisions. Which is another reason why you should get to know your professors and let them get to know you: they are more than just teachers and researchers. They, most of the time, have a heart and will do whatever they can to help you.

Family Resources

When you begin your college search, find out right away what your family and other people around you can do to help you with your college education. You want to find out what specifically they are willing to commit to and you want to be clear about it so there is no confusion down the road.

I have frequently heard stories about parents who assumed their kid was going to get the money by winning scholarships or just taking out loans and the kid overestimated their parents' financial ability and expected them or some other family member to help pay for their education. This lack of clarity causes a rift in families.

As I wrote in the section about relationships earlier, you have to ask questions but you cannot expect. However, when you ask questions, you reach clarity -- you know where you stand -- so that you can make a plan to bridge the gap. And when you walk into those conversations without expectations, you diminish a chance of getting hurt.

As a part of this conversation, you want to find out how much money will people specifically commit for four years of your education, if any. Are they willing to co-sign a loan for you? Will they offer to buy groceries or help in some other way? Can you live with them if you choose to attend a local school, and what would that arrangement be like? Again, be as clear as you can and if they are dodging the question, assume less than you'd like.

In fact, don't assume anything.

Sometimes, when people are able and willing to help you, they tell you straight out. It is often that when they don't want to or can't help you that they remain quiet. Give them the permission to be open by inviting them to do so without a threat of punishment or disappointment on your end.

It is really tough when you don't get the support, I know; but it even is harder when you don't know what you can expect; when expectations and commitments are blurry. On the other hand, when you make it happen on your own, independently and through hard work, the feeling of accomplishment is amazing and no one will ever take that way (although some people may try to take credit even when credit isn't due).

Get Creative

After I did not get the resident assistant job, I found myself facing a gap of between $8,000-10,000 a year. I was devastated. I had also just lost my job due to budgetary concerns -- or maybe because I challenged the system too much -- and I felt helpless. But then, after my pity-party was over, I began wondering where I could find the money to bridge the gap. My family was not an option, so I decided that the first step was to find a job for the remainder of the year (I found two) and then get a job for the summer and the fall.

I spent a lot of time explaining my situation to people, asking them for advice, asking them to help in some way and I tried to be grateful for all the help that I could get. I talked to professors, librarians, friends, and members of the college's Board of Trustees, and anyone else who wanted to listen.

For example, my freshman year, I did not have a computer, so a friend of mine lent me his; that made a huge difference and I will never forget his kindness. Also, it was a librarian who saw me moping around one day and took me aside, listened my plight, and then proceeded to give me a job the next day, after shuffling her budget around.

Those acts of kindness just reaffirmed my belief that people will do the right thing and help out whenever they can, and especially if they see that you are doing your part. On my end, I did not spend my time sleeping in and slacking in class; instead, I had all As and Bs, worked as many hours as I could, and volunteered thousands of hours. I also tried, the best I knew how, to explain how grateful I was -- and still am -- for all their help.

Would you help someone who is not really interested in putting in the work and expressing their gratitude? Me neither. Therefore, I would not have expected others to do any different.

When paying for college, most people think about the tuition expenses. However, there are many other fees that preclude people from attending, such as housing, food, books, student life and health fees, transportation, and just discretionary expenses.

Of course, when I was in high school, I lived with a host family, so I thought why not try to do the same over the winter and summer breaks. Thanks to my friendship with one my classmates, I was fortunate to be hosted by her parents during those two breaks. They were wonderful people who wanted to help and truly made a difference. Not only was I staying there, but also they would drive me places, pay for food, and do their best to make me feel at home and a part of the family. My "American Mom," as I called her, would even pack me lunches -- or, in my case, an overnight snack since I usually worked the night shift as the campus safety officer.

They understood the challenges I was facing, but they also saw that I was working hard and as best as I knew how to make things happen. I remember one particular occasion when I bought my first computer and some clothes ... I was so embarrassed, because I thought that they would think I was wasting money instead of saving it for school. Of course, they did not think that; they knew I was responsible, reliable, and not frivolous.

Another creative way of getting additional funding is by getting involved in student organizations. Most don't offer any compensation, but some do in form of stipends. Of course, unless you are truly interested in their mission and willing to put in the work, there's no way they will pick you for the job. For example, while at St. Norbert, I received stipends from the student government in my capacity as secretary and vice president and the newspaper while I served as the editor. However, there were several other organizations that offered stipends but I never applied for those "jobs" -- the connection wasn't there.

Finally, as my own scholarship, grant, and work options reached a limit, I also benefited from the generosity of several incredible individuals who helped me bridge the financial gap in college and then pay for most of my graduate school, too. I don't know if this was a divine intervention or just sheer luck, but without their help, I do not think I would have been able to complete my college degree or pursue graduate work.

These funding opportunities are fairly rare and, in my case, they came through conversations with others. I told people my story, my struggles, and asked if they could help or recommend someone who could. Most told me "you will be just fine" and went about their day, some offered true compassion, and a few had concrete suggestions. Their advice did not always work and most people I did ask for money said "no." However, I do believe that by working hard and finding myself in the right place, at the right time, and with the right attitude, I was able to land the kind of support that I needed. Beyond their dollars, these few individuals demonstrated their faith in me, and my potential for the future. This meant a lot to me and only inspired me even more.

Someone called all this: personal fundraising. Perhaps it is. The truth is, it is incredibly nerve-wracking and uncomfortable to ask for money for yourself. You are essentially asking for charity and you are asking that they believe in you, even though you have very little to give in return except a promise of your future accomplishments and that you will do the same for someone else, someday.

For a long time, I was very discreet about this because I did not think this was an accomplishment. I did not think I was doing something extraordinary, or being particularly smart. Rather, I was doing something that made sense within the context of my own circumstances. If you recall, I was not eligible for most of the things above: no outside scholarships, no "international student" grants, no loans, no option of working off-campus full-time, and no substantial money from my family. I needed alternatives.

Which brings me to my final point. When you ask yourself: how should I pay for college, the answer is: find a way. I don't know your particular situation, but look around you and instead of thinking of all the obstacles, look for opportunities. *Can you maybe start a business? What about a well-paid job? What school would offer you more money? Who can you ask to invest in you and your future? Can you write a better application for scholarships? What if you wrote a scholarship application every week for four years?* That's a total of 208 scholarship applications. The odds would be in your favor to win at least one.

In either case, just keep pushing, because if I was able to find the money against all odds, nothing says that you wouldn't be able to do the same. Don't settle for loans, if you don't have to, and exhaust all other options first. Work hard and explore all alternatives.

If you want an education – and are determined to make the most out of it, as best as you know how – in one way or another, it will happen for you.

18. INTERNATIONAL STUDENTS AND AMERICAN EDUCATION

When in Rome, do as the Romans do.
LATIN PROVERB

I debated a lot whether I should write this chapter to highlight international students and their unique educational journey in the United States, because most of the things included in this book already apply to pretty much anyone. That said, I recognized that there are several lessons that have benefited me greatly and you may find useful.

1. Become proficient in the language. I have met some internationals who have a very hard time with becoming fluent in English. This can be tough. It is really difficult to connect with people, open doors, and ultimately succeed if you cannot understand each other. I am not saying that your language skills have to be perfect; even to this day, I still make mistakes with the "article" usage (there are no articles in the Montenegrin language), which I am sure you have noticed throughout this book. What I am really talking about is being able to effectively communicate. If people just nod their heads or keep asking you "what did you say?" or, ever worse, look confused, please, please, please put in the effort to improve your skills. You will also feel a lot more comfortable and included. Finally, if people cannot understand you, they will have a very hard time trusting you and that's a shame.

2. When in Rome... I am all for authenticity, but it was you who chose to come here and attend school. Immerse yourself into the culture and its people. The first gift I received after coming to the United States, and to Wisconsin in particular, was the Green Bay Packers hat. I am a big Packer fan to this day. Respect and learn to appreciate local rituals for what they are.

3. Do not become a part of "a clique." This is so easy to do. International students hang out with international students and English as Second Language students hang out with each other; Asians with Asians; Europeans with Europeans. This is a very natural outcome when you come to a new country: you gravitate to that which is familiar to you and people that you feel will understand you best and that you have a common bond with. The problem with this is that you isolate yourself, so your cultural immersion and language learning suffers.

If you make a choice to come to America, you may look back with a great melancholy on the old country, but you are now in the New World. You have brought the old ways with you, but you have to merge them with the new culture and new people. Otherwise, you will always be an outsider ... and if you are an international student, you know how difficult and painful this can be at times.

4. Relax and laugh at yourself. When I went to Taco Bell for the first time, my sister tried to explain to me what some of the things were -- including their names. Taco Bell was completely new to me and I didn't want to sound stupid, so I was very stressed out during the whole experience. On the other hand, if we had just laughed at my weird pronunciations, life would have been much easier. At another occasion, while having dinner at a restaurant, my host mom asked me if I would be interested in helping her prepare some gifts for Christmas; enthusiastically I proclaimed: "Of course! I love raping presents!"

I can still remember the look at the waiter's face!

What you do? I had heard the word "rape" before, but did not necessary understand what it meant and it seemed close enough to "wrap," so I said it. While you are learning the language, these type of gaffes are common; laugh at it because, it is funny and, in reality, it means you are learning.

5. Take pride in your heritage, but do not dismiss that of others. In other words, you should definitely be proud of your heritage. But if you sound like you are more proud of your old country than of your new one, why are you here then? This may sound harsh, but think of it in reverse: if you were back in your home country and an American came over and just kept talking how awesome America is, wouldn't you get bored by it? I made this mistake when I first came; I missed people that I had left behind and was lonely, so I made Montenegro sound like the best thing since apple pie. Don't make the same mistake.

6. Be in on the joke. Humor helps us cope with difficulties in life and it also helps us understand life and other people better. People often use humor to connect with others as well. Sometimes, these jokes will be directed at you, too. And that's usually okay.

During my senior year of high school, in our U.S. '45 class, this guy started calling me FES: Foreign Exchange Student from *That 70's Show*. I had no idea what FES was nor where it came from, so I got defensive. Thankfully, the teacher explained what he was referring to, but by the time that happened, my chance of forming a friendship with this guy was gone. My inability to laugh at it and the fact that I got defensive embarrassed him. It is pretty trivial, but I think it bothered me for weeks back then.

It takes a lot of courage to leave the place of your origin in the pursuit of an education and a better life elsewhere. A lot of people are able to appreciate -- even admire -- that about you, and you should feel proud, as well, for that is a big accomplishment. I hope you can find it in you to enjoy every moment of your American experience.

PART FOUR
Career

19. TRANSLATING YOUR PURPOSE INTO A CAREER

> *I've learned that making a "living" is not the same thing as "making a life."*
> MAYA ANGELOU

Did you know that less than 25% of people in the United States love their jobs?

There's a reason for that.

For most of our lives, either by watching or being directly told, we have developed a belief that we work not because it is enjoyable, but because we need to as a means of survival. Consequently, many people acquire jobs that they don't' like, but they still do them while counting hours and minutes until the weekend. Then, when Sunday rolls around, they start feeling anxious and annoyed about Monday. Just think how many jokes are made about Mondays, not to mention everyone saying TGIF: Thank God It's Friday on Fridays.

What if we turned that around and looked for jobs that we enjoyed doing so much that we would be saying TGIM: Thank God It's Monday?! What if found jobs that we enjoyed, so that every new work week was just another opportunity to give of ourselves and contribute to the world?

This does not diminish the stress that comes with any job

or days when we are exhausted yet still need to show up for our shift; however, it would allow us to enjoy our work for the most part instead of spending weeks, months, and often years doing the stuff we dislike. Living a life where we spend so much time hating our jobs is torturous. It is also exhausting.

Think about it: there are 168 hours in a week and you spend at least 40 working (if you are employed full-time). Add to that the commute to and from work and all the hours you spend preparing for it -- and often agonizing about it -- and soon enough your job becomes your life. Not to mention that if you spend all that time doing something you hate, you will probably feel exhausted, unfulfilled, grumpy, annoyed, and fundamentally unhappy.

We all want our lives to have meaning, yet somehow most of us spend so much time doing the stuff that does the opposite: it kills the meaning.

What if I told you that it is possible for you to love and enjoy your work, 75% of the time? What if you could find the kind of work that enriches you and motivates you to do more of it? What if you could get up in the morning and never felt like you are working? What if you felt bad that you are getting paid for just living your life and doing what you love?

This kind of life is possible. Yes, it is possible for you to do the work you enjoy and still pay your bills. It is possible for you to enjoy your life and feel content at least 75% of the time. I tell you this, because I feel that way.

I love my social impact work. I love going to my co-working space and making things happen. I also love coaching, talking to people, being on the stage empowering others to do the same, and also writing this book, too. The fact that it is stressful, that our work at iOme Challenge work can be ...well... very challenging, that being an entrepreneur is incredibly uncertain, and that sometimes I encounter weeks of hitting a proverbial wall and keep hearing "no," does not change the fact that I wake up in the morning feeling that I am doing something that matters. Believe me, writing this book has been very stressful, but it has also been worth it, because once it is done, it has a potential to impact people's lives for the better. Which is both a reflection of my purpose and of my passions.

My experience with this is not singular. The 25% of people who do love their jobs agree with me. I have seen this in my coaching work, by reading other people's stories, or even spending time surrounded by the people who do pursue their passions. Ultimately, if it is possible for others, it is possible for you too.

It all begins with your purpose. *Why are you here?* If your work does not express your purpose, it is probably time for you to find something different to do. Similarly, *what are your passions?* Do you get to express those 75% of the time? If the answer is no, it is indeed time to do something else.

For me, my purpose of impacting the world and doing so through my passion of building organizations and empowering people is fully in line, so even if I was not working with iOme, I would find something else that resonates in a similar way. This is why you need to understand your purpose well. In terms of your work, you should do the same. Align your purpose and your passions with how you spend your days. Life is too short to spend it in misery if you have an opportunity to do more than that. And you do have that opportunity because you are alive and you are here, now.

Which brings me to my second point:

It all comes to fruition when you look at your life as one whole and not a collection of several pieces. In other words, people look at their job, their hobbies, their relationships, their chores, and their after-work activities as separate from each other. You have a professional and a personal life, the family life and the spiritual life, and so on. The reality is: they are not separate; they are all a part of one life -- your life.

Pursuing a job for the purposes of making money (yet calling it a career) without connecting it to the other areas of your life and your greater purpose does not work. It isolates you and keeps you confined -- and trapped -- in thinking that having that job is essential to your survival. It is not. All it does is limit you from seeing the bigger picture and recognizing your talents -- that go beyond any one particular job -- and your purpose; the reason why you are here in the first place.

Looking at your life as a collection of segments prevents you from taking a deep breath and grasping all that life has to offer. It prevents you from living a well integrated life, feeling content, and having meaning. So, when you look at your life as a whole, consider how you spend your days.

Are you living out your purpose in all spheres of your life? Are you expressing your passions? Are you spending 75% of your time engaging in the activities that are life giving. Are those activities fulfilling your purpose in some way?

If the answer is no, then step back and consider those 168 hours in your week and change the way you use them. Do more of that which reflects your purpose and expresses your passions.

Although I am sure you fulfill some of your passions to some degree (e.g. love going out, reading, watching TV, etc.), make sure you do the same with your purpose. I know, you are about to tell me that you have to pay your bills. I hear you. I have to pay my bills, too. I am not saying you should run away, become a Bohemian, and live by bartering goods and services. All I am saying is, discover what makes you tick and do that. If that cannot pay your bills, then still do that and find other ways to pay your bills. Even if you found a job that is rewarding 50% of the time, you would still be in a better shape than you are now. Don't settle for hating your existence -- hating a major part of your life -- because I have a curious feeling that you will regret it some day. Instead, find a way to spend your days doing more of the things you enjoy even if at first you are not paid for them.

For example, if you enjoy photography, you can have another job and still go out and take pictures, and do so daily. Who knows, maybe one day photography will pay your bills.

Same goes with any other field as long as it reflects your purpose, utilizes your passions, and matches with your talents (e.g. I can play basketball all I want, but I doubt I'd ever play for the Chicago Bulls!) The funny thing about this is that if your "hobby" does start to pay your bills, you won't even notice it, because that won't matter. What will matter is that you are doing it in the first place.

Most of us want comfortable lives. But what is also true is that unless we are living out our purpose, our lives-- regardless of the material means--will be miserable. We all know of an investment banker or an attorney who hates their job and finds little meaning in it, even though they make plenty of money. Similarly, we have also heard of a social worker who makes a lot less money than an attorney, but goes home feeling accomplished and rewarded. We live in the world where we are not cool enough if we work at a coffee shop and paint for a living, yet somehow it is okay for people to spend 40-50 hours a week hating their lives. In my opinion, this is ridiculous!

I have also observed that there's a simple solution to this: do what you love and the money will follow. I know it sounds cliché, but I really believe this is true and have witnessed it many times in my own life, through my work with people, and by observing others.

Each of us has come into this world with a set of talents, inclinations, and preferences. They are all different and ours are unique to us. We are blessed in a different way. But our purpose is not to survive, but to thrive by living out that which is within us.

Do not look for obstacles and limitations that suggest why you cannot live it out -- that is, quite frankly, easy to do and most people do it. If you look around, most people complain about something and we consistently engage in conversations about how busy we are and how stressful our jobs are. We say how we will leap into starting our own businesses, going back to school, writing a book, or finding a new job, but then we put a caveat that something first needs to happen for us to do that.

Maybe we need to have a safety net, or more time, or more money, and so on. Always something. Believe me, I am familiar with these excuses ... even this book was a desire of mine for a long time, but fear prevented me from publishing it. So, instead of just getting it done, I kept finding excuses.

The truth is, we give all these excuses because we are afraid of success – yes, success. It is easy to be miserable; we are used to that. It is much harder to embrace success and happiness, and keep it going. It leaves nothing to complain about. Which is more, it forces to change how we have lived our lives so far. And that change is scary.

We have been taught to fear, instead of to love. We have not been encouraged to claim our life in a way that will trigger our passions, which will in turn motivate us to defy the odds and do that which we enjoy. We have been taught to play it safe even if we feel miserable for the sake of security, which is not even a real thing: the planets, the Sun, and our entire solar system is consistently moving. Why would we think then that anything is constant? As I said earlier in the book, the only constant in life is change. Yet, paradoxically, that is one thing that we fear the most.

This does not have to be so. Have the courage to really understand your purpose, make a plan of living it out, and go for it. Set deadlines for yourself and announce it publically, as a way to holding yourself accountable. Test things out. Give something a shot; if it fails, try something else. There is no shame in going into the arena and fighting, it's only a pity if you sit by the sidelines wondering what could it could have been like.

You may not believe me, but I genuinely mean it when I say that there is no reason for you to not find a way to sing your song in one way or another. Don't let it die within you without giving it an honest try.

As Franklin Delano Roosevelt said,

"the only fear we have to fear is the fear itself."

20. LANDING A GIG

> *Choose a job that you like, and you will never*
> *have to work a day in your life. .*
> CONFUCIUS

My first job after college came only two days after graduation and it entailed turn around a nonprofit: The Richard Mauthe Center for Faith, Spirituality, and Social Justice. It was an exciting opportunity for a freshly minted college graduate to test out my leadership skills, explore various programmatic ideas, and raise some money for a worthy cause. It was also an opportunity to work with my mentor, who vowed to teach me all he knew; I learned a lot, managed people, and was quite successful as attested by the goals we achieved. What was so unique given my experience in the former Yugoslavia was that we worked to bring 11 faith traditions under the same roof embracing the postulates of peace, social justice, and respect. We understood that to work for common good, it required all of us to come together for the benefit of the young people we served.

This experience also proved to me that it is not only what you know and how much you know, but who you know. When looking for a job, if you want to be successful, you need to know what you are doing and, generally, you need to demonstrate that in some way. At the same time, all your knowledge may be useless if you don't have an opportunity to present it to someone.

For example, during my senior year of college, I applied to a lot of jobs at universities -- especially Ivy League schools -- because I was hoping to get a job that would come with tuition benefits, which would in turn help me get a Master's degree. This, of course, never happened and in large part because I had no connections at those places that could have helped me land an interview.

However, once you know people -- especially people who know your character, your track record, and your capacity -- many opportunities will present themselves. At the same time that I took the job at the Mauthe Center, I was offered another one at a for-profit firm because a member of St. Norbert Board of Trustees made a referral. It was in this same vein how iOme Challenge was started. My former professor called to talk about how we might get college students involved to think and talk about long-term financial security and its impact on the social and economic well-being of our society. My work with the American Library Association and the Association of College and Research Librarians happened in the similar manner. One relationship leads to another and when one door opens, the other usually follows. A lot of us spend a lot of time doing activities that produce little results. This is especially true with job-searches. We keep on searching, yet we are not very deliberate and strategic about it. Which is why most of us don't get all the jobs we apply for.

With that said, here are some tips that I think work better when it comes to landing the first, the second, or the ninth gig:

1. Be Prepared: I recently heard a story about a young woman in her 20s, who came to an interview and handed a resume with words "sorry, the printer didn't work." The formatting of the resume was completely messed up. *Would you hire someone like that?* I wouldn't. The least you can do is format your resume properly. Properly means that it is well-organized, in a logical and easily comprehended manner; you don't want an employer to be hunting for your credentials ... because they *won't*. Make sure there are no typos. Use clear and direct language. And don't try to pull the wool over anyone's eyes; tell what you have done with conviction.

Sincerity and passion to learn and do well will help you a lot more than false confidence and large font to fill the page.

When you go to an interview make sure that you are prepared. Read up on the organization and the people that will be interviewing you, dress properly, be articulate and ask good questions. If I am hiring an intern or a staff member, I want to see their potential and their capacity for success. If you did not take enough time to understand what the organization is about or how to pronounce my name, what makes you think I would believe you when you say that you would do a good job? Also, you should probably look me up and know that I am a guy. I once interviewed someone who came in and asked for me as "Ms. Redzic."

The best way to be prepared is to actually have a track record. Those internships I was talking about earlier; independent studies with your professors; independent projects or well-written papers that you can share with your prospective employer. Volunteer experiences. That's the stuff people look for when hiring.

If you were a member of some organization without any specific work you did, you won't get far. But, if you actually volunteered because you wanted to learn something -- and you actually did learn something -- I am interested. In either case, if you are looking for a job, make sure to have enough to show that matches what the company is looking for and demonstrates that you are a good fit. Not just because you say so, but because you can convince your prospective boss that it is true (talking about it won't convince anyone; doing it will).

Of course, if you have actually held a full-time job, you

can talk about what you have done before. Keep in mind though: when people are hiring, they want to know what you can do for them and how well you can do it. So, focus on transferrable skills (e.g. the fact you had a million dollars marketing budget at the old place is not transferrable; your extraordinary writing skills and connections are).

Finally, more than anything: show passion for working in that job, at that particular organization, and tie it to your purpose. If you do so in a genuine and persuasive way, you are likely to land a job. We all want to work with people who wake up in the morning and feel they are doing what they are called to do. We especially want those people at our organizations.

2. Relationships Matter: As I illustrated in the beginning of this chapter and throughout this book: relationships matter. In fact, they are often critical in helping you land a job you will love. They can be helpful by opening doors, service as a reference, or actually hiring you or referring you directly to someone else, and so on.

As you look for a new job, consider the people you know and in what ways they can help you advance your career. You would help them, right? And a lot of people will help you too. This is especially true if you are just out of college. Talk to your faculty; many of them know a lot of people or have their own businesses. Look at the list of your college's alumni and reach out to those that you believe can help. Consider people you may have met along the way, either in college or earlier, and reach out. As long as you have left a good impression, they would probably be happy to hear from you.

Depending on the job or the organization you are apply at, you may also want to look at their list of employees, members of the board, and even interns. You never know who knows whom. This is especially true in smaller communities. Social tools like LinkedIn can be helpful in connecting with people, or at least understanding their networks. Sometimes, though not really recommended, you can even drop a name thus borrowing the credibility of a mutual connection. In either case, as you have learned before in the section on relationships, building your own community is really important, in general; but when it comes to getting a job, your community may prove essential.

3. Find Opportunity: Perhaps this belongs in the chapter on entrepreneurship, but I believe that to be successful we need to always look for opportunities and connect the dots, for ourselves and for others. When I was asked to get involved with iOme -- even before we had the name for it -- I jumped at it, because I love service and new ventures. I also saw an enormous need and potential for it. In other words, I saw an opportunity to make an impact.

When you are looking for a new job, considering changing your career, or want to execute a project, don't focus on the obstacles, but rather consider all possible solutions to your dilemma. Life is rarely a straight line, so you need to be on the look out for the creative solutions that have not been explored -- or even happened -- before. For example, what if you can see a particular need for your current company and suggest it to your boss. Maybe the company needs a new department, or a new product, or a new process in order to be more successful. Or, maybe someone during conversation at a dinner party mentions that they have a particular problem that they need to be solved; maybe you can be the person who solves it for them.

When you are on a lookout for opportunities, you will begin seeing more and more of them every day. You will recognize gaps that you can fill, issues you can address, and causes you can enhance. Focus on your purpose, but remain flexible how you live it out. You never know when the right opportunity might struck.

For example, a younger friend of mine has always dreamed of working for the United Nations, but in his head, this was something that would happen later in his life. He felt this way, because he thought he would need all these experiences before they would ever hire him. He was so convinced of this that when he was offered an internship there recently, he almost declined (he almost declined his dream opportunity— something he wanted for a long, long time) because of a few obstacles!

Always look for opportunity, ignore fear, and then "hire" your brain to figure out how to make it come to life.

America is the land of opportunity.

To take that one step further, life is one *big* opportunity.

Seize it.

21. DOING YOUR OWN THING

The best way to predict the future is to create it.
PETER DRUCKER

I believe that some people are hard-wired to draw outside of the box. They hate limitations, especially those imposed in the context of a job. They hate having to come in to work at 8 am and leave at 5 pm, with only an hour for lunch. They hate not being able to text when they want to or check YouTube on their work computer when they feel like it. They feel stifled by the rules and regulation, and limited with bureaucracy. They view micro-management, top-down approach, a lack of encouragement, and a culture of fear as sure ways of making lives miserable.

They want to get up in the morning and fight a good fight, for a cause they believe in and in service of their passions. They believe that creativity will save the world and that life is about offering solutions to particular needs or challenges, both individual and societal. They believe in harnessing the power of human ingenuity to deliver what other people think is impossible.

They are intuitive leaders, who have the ability to motivate people, and to get things done. They are square pegs in the round holes whose brains operate differently than those of others.

They feel so strongly about pursuing their own thing that they are willing to wrestle with uncertainty and long hours. They may be stressed, yet always having fun. They are willing to try, and fail, and try again, and fail again, until something sticks. And if nothing sticks, they will try again. They will try something entirely different.

These are leaders. They are innovators. They are visionaries.

They are independent minds who like doing their own thing. Not because they think they know better than everyone else (quite to the contrary: best of them realize how little they know); rather, it is because they can't help themselves. They have an idea, they have a vision, they have an urge, an inspiration, and they go for it.

They don't do well with being limited by the lack of imagination of their bosses or their society.

If this sounds like you keep reading.

I believe that we all have a little bit of this leadership; this innovation; and this entrepreneurial madness in ourselves. This is called creativity. A desire to put our own touch on things. Build something new. Find solutions. Lead an effort. Change the world.

Many of us want this freedom at some level. However, some of us fear to venture into the unknown while others feel limited by their circumstances. We fear embarrassment. Ridicule. A failure.

I wanted to include a chapter about entrepreneurship to encourage you to follow that itch and give yourself a chance to start something new. To do your own thing. Create a future that you want. To risk some effort, and some money, and see if you enjoy it.

Create something and send it off to the world. Shove it out there and say, "Hello, world! Look! I made this! I love it! And, if you don't, I don't care!"

There is a lot -- a lot -- written about entrepreneurship,

social entrepreneurship, and leadership in general to fill an entire library. But, for the purposes of this book, I wanted to encourage you to pursue your entrepreneurial zeal in some capacity. It is tough, it is complicated, it can be enormously difficult, and very uncertain, but the sense of freedom you obtain is worth all the struggle. The sheer experience is wroth it.

One thing that separates good entrepreneurs and good leaders from great ones is courage. The daring to push the limits and shoot in the dark with a conviction. A desire to try... and keep on doing it over, and over, and over again.

I have read a lot on the topic of both leadership and entrepreneurship; some of it, I retained. Other stuff, I still need to re-learn. However, these are a few lessons that I believe will offer some inspiration as you -- provided you do -- embark on this quest and answer the call of entrepreneurial madness.

1. If you want to make money, don't get into entrepreneurship. You may strike big -- we all would like to strike big -- but you don't become an entrepreneur because that's a safe and a certain path to riches.

2. You must love what you do. Your entrepreneurship venture needs to align with your purpose and passions, otherwise you will quit the moment you encounter the first obstacle.

3. Social Entrepreneurs are called that because they are addressing a social issue. They don't say that as a marketing ploy nor are they willing to sacrifice the mission in exchange for higher earnings.

4. Don't just shuffle the information and ideas and then pass them on to others. Try to create some new content and solutions, too.

5. Have the courage to try and fail, and the perseverance to keep going.

6. Be your biggest fan and keep cheering on. At the same time, develop a tight group of people around you who can cheer you on, too.

7. Entrepreneurs have to understand the basics of marketing, management, sales, production, administration, human resources, law, technology, and everything in-between that's relevant to their effort. They may not have to do it all, but they definitely don't have a department or a budget in their start-up that can handle that.

8. Remember: Chinese characters for the word crisis consist of danger and opportunity. With every danger, comes opportunity.

9. Vision is paramount, passion is essential, and execution is key.

10. Stay positive. Stay optimistic. Take care of yourself. Don't let negativity and negative people kill your spirit and drive.

PART FIVE
Money

22. WHY WE DON'T MANAGE MONEY AND WHY WE SHOULD

Money is a terrible master,
but an excellent servant.
P. T. BARNUM

After considering the enormous student loan debt, which has long surpassed $1 trillion, the credit card debt, and the long-term financial challenges that my generation, the so-called Millennials, will face down the road, I was compelled to dedicate an entire section on money. Having an understanding of debt, and student debt at that, is only a portion of what people refer to as "financial literacy" or "financial capability." In these couple of chapters, I will outline some basic money lessons that are essential to a successful life.

I believe that for many of us, happiness is a matter of choice, not circumstance. However, when our basic needs aren't met, it is difficult to focus on much beside our basic survival. And, in the world where money plays a critical role in assuring that survival, it is paramount that we learn how to manage our finances.

Unfortunately, conversations about money can be very uncomfortable for many people. Perhaps you are one of those people. Perhaps you would rather discuss other people's money -- especially people who have a lot of money -- instead of your own money and the problems you have with it.

How much debt do you have? Do you file your taxes every year? What is your credit score? Are you paying high interest rates? Are you able to save? Are you cashing checks for a fee instead of having them direct-deposited? The list of questions goes on.

A big reason why we don't talk about money has to do with culture. This is especially true in the United States, where for a long time and for many people, money was not a big object of concern. At least, not an *open* topic of concern. Many parents focused on assuring that their children have better lives than them, so they chose to not burden their kids with money issues.

Have your parents talked to you about money? Do you know how much they made, how much they saved, and have they taught you to do the same?

If the answer to these questions is a "no," or "I don't know," that is a good sign that you, too, were a victim of this culture.

As one of iOme Challenge's contest winners said once: "it will take a generation to change a generation, because an entire generation never learned how to manage their money." While it may take a generation to affect cultural change, I believe that each of us can take responsibility for our own finances, today. More to the point, it is not only about "being able to take responsibility," but rather: it is essential that we do so. This is, of course, if you appreciate freedom of choice and wish to obtain -- and maintain -- even an average quality of life.

For some of us, money conversations happened because we had no other choice. I was fortunate to have parents who always spoke about finances openly; in poverty and in wealth alike. These conversations were difficult at times, especially those times when I desired something but we couldn't afford it. Perhaps those conversations were too big of a burden to carry for a kid of my age. However, they also made talking about money much easier later on.

For example, I have no problem discussing money with those close to me, telling them about my financial situation, and even sharing my money struggles, including those times when I had to hunt for quarters around my apartment to buy food. Unfortunately, those times have been many, but there is no shame in not having money (or having money, for that matter); however, we still need to take responsibility for our own financial well-being. Even though it may seem that way, you do not have to be wealthy to get a financial advisor who can help you invest and save your money or to go online and play with financial calculators, read articles on finance, and talk to others about it.

Taking responsibility means that you take the time to understand how credit works, know your financial obligations, live within your means as best as you can and even as you work to increase them, and save for the future. It also means that you do not ignore financial problems, because they only get bigger over time. It means that you talk about money freely and openly. It means that you ask for help when you need it and avoid pretending you have it all under control when you don't. Or nod your head when someone mentions financial terms that you don't understand. I vividly remember a Realtor telling me once "the place is great too, because they also let you pay your rent with a credit card without charging you the APR." I looked at her and smiled, realizing that she had no idea what APR (Annual Percentage Rate) stood for and that it has nothing to do with the processing fee that she was actually talking about.

I get it. Money conversations can be very uncomfortable and intimidating, especially when we are broke. But they are - - I can't stress this enough -- essential for your financial health, and by extension the quality of your life. Our individual money habits also affect the society as a whole. For example, when we talk about retirement among Millennials, we are not concerned about the percentage of this generation that will save for retirement; we are concerned about all the others who won't and will thus affect the social and economic well being of our country as a whole. Individual financial capability has a direct impact on all of us.

The following chapters are lessons that I have found most helpful in managing my money, but they are not an all-inclusive, one-size-fits-all answer and they may not work for you (though I think they will). There are many other resources out there. Make sure to check those out to. I also strongly encourage you to save for retirement and speak out about the importance of financial security in our later years.

23. MANAGING YOUR MONEY

Money seems a lot more difficult than it should be and is often over-complicated by terminology, acronyms and the like. I won't get into the evolution of the financial sector, and how we got here from the barter economy of our ancestors. However, the gist of it is: you work (i.e. provide goods and services) in exchange for something. Back in the day, that something may have been a roof over your head and food. Then, it became silver and gold. Today, it is "money," a concept that we place value on. When we receive money by providing goods and services, we are receiving income. When we spend that income to obtain what we need or want, that is an expense.

Income v. Expense
If you bring in $100/month and spend $100, you are at 0. If you spend $80, you can make the $20 you have left work for you in the future through saving and/or investing. If you spend $120, you are indebting yourself thus causing a burden on yourself in the future. Ideally, you will not spend $100. If

you have to spend $100, try not to spend $120, unless you have a way of paying it back right away or if a situation is dire. If you earn 100 and spend 100, your budget is balanced. But, what is budget?

Budget

Budget is your income and expense plan over a specific period of time. *Do you have one?* This is an essential step in managing your money: outlining what your income will be, what your projected expenses are, and the difference between the two. Without a budget, you cannot see a big picture of your finances and thus be responsible with it, and maximize it. This is an example of a budget that I use; values are fictional:

Sample Monthly Budget	
Income	
Gross Income	$3,500
Income Taxes	$400
Social Security Taxes	$268
Net Income	**$2,832**
Dedicated Savings	
Retirement Savings	$200
Emergency Savings	$75
Total Savings	**$275**
Dedicated Expenses	
Rent	$1,250
Renter's Insurance	$20
Car Payment	$250
Car Insurance	$50
Fuel	$125
Groceries	$300
Total Dedicated Expenses	**$1,995**
Discretionary Expenses	
Clothing	$100
Dining Out	$150
Hobbies	$50
Cash Withdrawals	$100
Total Discretionary Expenses	**$400**
Monthly Cash Surplus	**$162**

There are a lot of ways and formats that you can use to outline your budget. Essentially, however, you want to list your expenses, your income, and see what the difference is. From there on, you want to shift things around (i.e. spend less) in order to achieve your financial goals.

Debt

Debt can come from a number of sources: overspending, student loans, credit cards, car loans, home mortgage, etc. Generally, unless you are fortunate to receive a no-interest loan from your friends or family, loans accrue interest. Interest is the amount you pay for using the loan, and each loan has a particular set of terms. That is to say, if you signed up for a student loan, you likely signed a "promissory note," a legal document saying that the loan provider will give you a certain amount of money upfront, or in installments, so that you can pay for your school; in turn, you promise to repay the loan within a specific amount of time at a certain interest rate. The interest you pay is how lending institutions and, in the case of federal student aid, the government make money.

Debt isn't all bad, of course. Borrowing money allows us to pursue our dreams and advance ourselves. For example, without the ability to borrow from the government and private lending institutions, many people may not have had a chance to attend college. Corporations and small businesses also borrow money in order to pay for new products, expansion, or to avoid cash flow issues, a situation where they have bills to pay but not enough money on hand. In order to make sure they pay their bills on time, businesses borrow money. Cash flow issues also happen to individuals, too. Entrepreneurs are especially notorious for this, since their income fluctuates so much and, given the size of most startups, cash reserves (or savings) are limited and often nonexistent.

Now, when borrowing money from financial institutions, you are extended a line of credit. What this means is that a bank, for example, deems you trustworthy to repay a particular amount of money, therefore they extend that amount in the form of a credit line for your use to cover certain expenses. When determining your ability to repay the loan, lending institutions review your credit worthiness. That is to say, financial institutions assess what their risk is in giving us the money. The higher the risk, the less likely it is they will lend us the cash. If they do, they will increase interest rates. The logic is simple: if they are taking a bet on us that we will pay the borrowed money back in a timely fashion, they want to at least make the risk worthwhile and make money while doing it.

Another, more structured, way of looking at this process is:

1. You apply for a loan with a lending institution.

2. They review your credit worthiness and ability to repay the loan to determine how much of a risk they are taking by extending a line of credit to you.

3. They extend a line of credit to you with a promissory note, with promises from both sides, outlining the terms of the loan agreement. When you get a loan, make sure to read this note carefully.

4. You use the money for whatever you need it for.

5. You pay it back by making payments according to the terms of the loan as outlined in the promissory note.

In sum, borrowing money is not inherently bad. It is only bad in the following case scenarios:

(a) When we borrow for things that we do not need;

(b) When we borrow even though we know with certainty that we cannot afford to pay back;

(c) When we borrow and have no reasonable expectation that we would be able to repay the loan; this expectation needs to be based in reality;

(d) When we borrow with a high interest rate (e.g. payday loans);

(e) When we borrow and default on our loans (e.g. do not pay back on time)

In other words, do not borrow money unless you have a reasonable expectation, rooted in past experiences, facts, or high odds that you will be able to pay it back. Of course, sometimes, we need to borrow money even if we aren't sure how exactly we will pay it back, like in the case of emergencies. Which is where the critical lesson in borrowing money comes: *if you do borrow money, make sure you pay it back* as soon as you can. This is especially true if your loan comes with a high interest rate.

Of course, there are situations in which the urgency to pay a loan off is not so dire, like in the case of mortgage, and it may make more sense to use the money available for something else. Also, remember that loan payments can be deferred or reduced if you are having financial difficulties, so make sure to speak with a financial advisor, a banker, or a financial coach (or whoever gave the loan) instead of defaulting on your loan.

Compound Interest

Compound interest is a mathematical formula, which calculates interest on top of already earned interest. That is to say, if you put $1,000 in savings, which represents "the principal," at an annual interest rate of 10% (the rate at which interest is calculated), you will have $1,100 at the end of the first year. If compound interest is at play, after the second year, you will have $1,210 (as opposed to only $1,200 if only simple interest were calculated). After the third year, you will have $1,331, and so on. When interest "compounds," you are earning interest on both the principal you invested and the interest you have earned so far. When calculating "simple interest," you would only earn interest on the principal amount invested each year.

The chart below shows the difference between compound and simple interest earnings using the example discussed above:

Difference Between Compound and Simple Interest Earnings			
Year	Original Principal Invested	Simple Interest Earnings	Compound Interest Earnings
0	$1,000	$0.00	$0.00
1	$1,000	$100.00	$100.00
2	$1,000	$100.00	$110.00
3	$1,000	$100.00	$121.00
4	$1,000	$100.00	$133.10
Total Interest Earned		$400.00	$464.10

It is said that Albert Einstein thought of compound interest as the most powerful human invention. If you have heard the expression "time value of money," it comes from the idea that the value of a dollar can increase (due to investment) or decrease (due to inflation) over time. Because of compound interest, the longer your money is being compounded, the more will you have in the long run. This is also another reason why it is so important that we begin saving (and investing) young, no matter how small our contributions. Another aspect of compound interest is that it is often calculated more than once a year, thus creating a higher effective percentage rate (EPR). For example, if your loan's APR is 12% compounded monthly (growing at 1% per month), your effective rate will actually be over 12% annually. This is why when investing or getting a loan, it is helpful to look at both: the interest rate and the compounding frequency.

The problem with compound interest is that it also applies to debt. So, the longer we hold debt, which compounds interest, the more interest we will pay. Another catch with debt, especially with credit cards, is that interest rates are generally higher than in case of savings accounts or even average investments. What this means for you is that if you have a $1,000 on one credit card with APR of 14% and $2,500 on another card with APR of 24%, make sure to first pay off the one with higher interest. This is not intuitive, because the sense of accomplishment that comes from paying off an entire loan is great; however, financially it makes sense to do so. Why? Higher interest rate means you are paying more money in the end.

24. CREDIT CARDS

> *Procrastination is like a credit card: it's a lot of*
> *fun until you get the bill.*
> CHRISTOPHER PARKER

Credit cards can be great for a number of reasons: many offer rewards in the form of travel perks, cash-back, merchandise gifts, etc; they are helpful in emergencies; you are not liable for any of unauthorized charges; and they can help build your credit (more on credit later). However, they are not so great if you do not manage them properly, because they can bury you in debt that you may end up paying for many, many years to come.

Credit cards are notorious for having high interest rates and many charge penalties if you do not pay your bill on time. I've encountered a situation where being late even a few hours caused a problem and I was charged $36 fee. Their "minimum payment" can be deceiving and you end up paying a lot in interest. Also, there seems to be overwhelming number of different credit card options, and everyone has an opinion on "which one is the best," their reward plans change frequently, and even your rate, credit terms, and credit limit can change without much notice.

To avoid getting into trouble with credit cards, these are a few rules of thumb:

1) Do not max out your credit cards...unless you absolutely have to. I have done this in the past because that was my only somewhat comfortable route of survival at the time. However, this should be your last resort because of astronomical interest rates and fees that you may end up paying, which also can have tremendous negative effects your credit.

2) Do not make late payments, because if you do, you may get hit by very high charges (depending on your credit card) that aren't necessary and will push you even deeper in your debt. But even if you do happen to be late, because, life happens, make sure to...

3) Always make a payment, even the minimum, because if you don't, they may report the absent payment to a credit reporting agency and then you have a much bigger problem. I am serious; if you have to skip a meal or two, or eat P&J sandwiches for a week, do it, but do not allow yourself to default on your credit card because that will haunt you for a long time. Of course, there is always an option of calling and asking for a short extension, which they may accommodate sometimes.

4) Pay off the highest interest cards first, because that will save you money in the long run. Once, I was in a situation where I owed about $4,000 on one card with 24.99% APR and $500 on another with 14.66% APR. I had about $600 that I could put toward my cards. I wanted to pay the smaller one off, badly, but that would have made little sense, as the card with the larger balance would have generated a much larger amount of interest. The point of the story: pay high interest loans first.

5) Avoid, if you can, paying one credit card with

another through balance transfers. While this is much better than holding on to a high balance at a higher interest rate, it is not a permanent solution.

6) If you take a 0% APR deal, make sure to pay it off in full, because you may end up getting hit by retroactive interest. Just like most people, I am no stranger to impulsive "swipe the card" purchases.

At one particular occasion, I opened a Best Buy credit card and purchased over $3,000 in gadgets (e.g. new laptop, TV, iPad, etc.). "I need it," I told myself and signed up for Best Buy's 18-month 0% APR promo. 6-, 12-, 18-, or 24-month promos are a way for businesses to entice customers to purchase their products. In turn, they give them a line of credit without interest for a specific period of time. This can be a great help if you need to purchase something; let's say, your computer dies and you really need it. However, it is not wise to do this unless you are absolutely sure you can pay it off within the promotional period.

In my case, I did not go blindly into my Best Buy purchases. I needed a new laptop for school and I calculated, in my head, that if I made 18 payments of $166.66, I would be set. In fact, I had planned on making higher payments so that I can pay it off within a year. I was stoked! Except, six months later, things did not work out this way and I found myself struggling to make even minimum payments. As I struggled to pay for food, maxed my other cards, and so on, it never occurred to me that the retroactive interest would kick in ... until I was hit by $780 on top of my already high balance. Needless to say, it was horrible. I have paid it off since, but I have learned my lesson and wish I realized what "retroactive interest" would actually do.

Learn from my mistake.

7) Do not have more than one credit card ... unless you know what you are doing. For example, I have more than one card and there are several benefits to this. Mainly, I use different cards for different purposes. For example, I have a "food" card which gives me points for restaurants; I have a card that I use for travel because I get insurance with it; some cards offer cash back rewards for certain purchases; store credit cards can provide the owner with discounts; the list of rewards offered by certain credit cards is numerous. The key here is to be *very active* in managing your cards, making sure to not miss payments and watching that your balances stay within manageable levels.

A very close friend of mine who is a financial guru advised me to not give you this advice, because most people get screwed over by having more than one credit card. *If you are not 100% sure you know what you are doing, listen to her, not me.* It is very easy to get burnt by having several cards.

8) Pay your balance off every month (if you can): I was recently giving a talk on financial and personal empowerment at Washington University in St. Louis, as a part of their financial literacy efforts during the annual Money Smart Week initiative, when I was approached by a mother/daughter duo who had some questions about credit cards, credit scores, and loans. In a stimulating conversation that followed, I learned that both of them have been told by their friends to keep the balance on their cards as a way to build credit. While I will address credit later on, it is essential that you remember: nothing good comes from carrying a credit card balance! Some financial gurus suggest carrying an occasional small balance as a way to increase your credit score; however, your credit score is determined by multiple factors greater than revolving a small and occasional balance on your credit card. I suggest always repaying the total balance, but if you can't pay the balance in full.

9) Pay as much as you can, because the more you pay, the lower will your principal be and thus lower your interest payment. Make a larger payment on your card every month even if you need to use it right away to pay your other bills. I used to pay my phone bill with a credit card right after making a payment on my card. This enabled me to lower the amount that interest would be calculated on. Typically, if you leave a balance on your card past your statement due date, interest will accumulate DAILY. By paying down the balance before it rolls into the next statement period, you lower the growing interest to be paid. That said, if you can, don't play this game at all. Just keep making the highest payments possible on your card until your balance is gone completely.

Finally,

10) Credit cards can be very beneficial in helping you avoid cash flow issues, gain cash back and earn points, and avoid possible overdrafts, bounced checks, and consequent fees on your checking account. You are better off using a credit card instead of depleting your checking account to less than $20. This is especially true if you can find a card with low interest or interest free for 18 months. Of course, in a perfect world, we would all have plenty of money, live within our means, save 20%, give away 10%, and live happily ever after. This, however, is not a reality for most of us. If you are living from a paycheck to paycheck, but pay your bills on time, don't carry any (or much) debt, and are responsible with money, it may make sense for you to get a credit card and charge all your monthly expenses on it.

First, you will get the points. But, more importantly, you will have peace of mind that you are not depleting your cash reserves or exposing yourself to potential fees. Unfortunately, back in the day, I tried to be extra responsible and only used my debit card, until I forgot about some charges that appeared late and was hit by $34 overdraft fee by my bank. Twice in one day. The amounts of overdraft were $0.02 and $4.35. That said, this advice only applies if you pay your card off every month, or--at the very least--you are able to pay it off within the next few months. Naturally, if you see yourself spending so much that you can't catch up, you need to slow down as this "paying for things on credit" strategy may not work for you. And, of course, if you fear overdraft, you can always get a checking account with a bank or credit union that offers you an overdraft line of credit and/or no fees if you overdraft.

Even though many of us have a solid understanding of these "rules of thumb" regarding credit cards, still, according to the 2013 iOme Challenge "Measure of Millennials" study, 37% of 18-32 year olds reported that they max out their credit cards and only 37% always pay their credit card balances in full. In my opinion, there are two main reasons for this: (1) credit cards have become a tool for survival rather than a tool for emergencies and credit-building; and, (2) a lack of knowledge concerning how to properly manage credit cards.

25. STUDENT LOANS

*Private student loans should be avoided
at all costs.*
SUZE ORMAN

At heart, student loans were a wonderful idea, giving millions of Americans an opportunity to obtain an education. However, with an astronomical increase in tuition and other college-related fees (over 75% in the last 10 years), the use of loans to fund education has grown exponentially and created a major burden for individuals and society alike. The Consumer Financial Protection Bureau (CFPB) reports that nearly 2/3 of all student loans are owed by those under 40 years of age. With over $1 trillion in student debt, this poses a serious problem. While we can argue the merits of these loans, the fairness of interest rates charged by the government, or the action the U.S. Congress could potentially take in order to eliminate debt or lessen the burden, the reality is that defaulting on your debt obligations can bear grave consequences for your long-term financial health (e.g. ability to buy a house, car, etc.)

Much like with credit card or any other debt, it is essential that we learn how to manage our student loans, come up with a plan to pay them off, and understand--fully understand--

what happens if we don't. That promissory note we signed is a legally binding document that will remain with us until we meet our obligations. A few years ago, a generous benefactor, without whom neither my college nor my graduate education would have been possible, asked if I would consider signing a promissory note to pay her back should she decide to lend as opposed to just give me the money. I happily said "yes," not realizing that a "promissory note" was actually a legal document. Thankfully, in my case, she was gracious to simply help me out and my debt to her goes beyond financial, and it will last a lifetime. However, if you signed a promissory note, you cannot take it lightly and just go with a flow. You need a plan. You need a commitment, with one goal in mind: paying it off. Do not harbor illusions that the government or anyone else will save you. While this is possible, it is contrary to the premise of responsibility and could affect other areas of your financial life.

Accordingly, here are some "rules of thumb" for student loans:

1) Understand how much you owe and your interest rates. The private loans you may have obtained from financial institutions (as opposed to government) sometimes have higher interest rates. Make sure to understand which loan has which interest rate, because...

2) Pay off the highest interest loans first in order to avoid paying a lot more in interest over time. Much like with credit cards, even if one of your loans is lesser in amount than the other and you could pay it off quicker, always focus on paying off the one with higher interest rate;

3) Pay more than the minimum, because this will help you pay less interest over time, get rid of your loans sooner thus reach freedom and have more money to spend on other things in the future, and it will give you a great sense of accomplishment. In other words, do your best to pay more than your minimum. Usually, there are no limits on how much you can pay monthly, so even if you can add $25 on top of your regular minimum payment, it will make a difference and you will be glad you did it in the long run.

4) Avoid student loan debt-relief services, because why in the world would you pay more money than you already have to? Debt in general and student loans in particular can be very overwhelming and scary. I understand that. However, hiring someone else to manage your debt for a hefty fee is neither wise nor responsible. You may think you are releasing the responsibility, but you are really not, because it is you who will end up paying for it all, anyway. Instead of falling into a trap of false advertising such as "you may be eligible for debt forgiveness," spend time understanding the terms of your loan and read up on student loans on the Department of Education website. Consumer Financial Protection Bureau also has helpful information, as does your local library or your college's financial aid office. While far from perfect and in many ways limited, government agencies, libraries, nonprofits, and financial aid offices can be helpful to you, for free. It is their mission to assist people and offer adequate and truthful information. I strongly urge you to explore free learning opportunities and to actually spend time looking at the forms and information. You may be surprised how straightforward some of this stuff can be.

5) Explore repayment options and government programs, because they can make your loan repayment a lot easier. You can be put on a schedule where you pay your loans back based on your income or you can even qualify for government programs where debt can indeed be forgiven. For example, a friend of mine has about $300,000 in student loan debt. She is an attorney. She also was smart enough to sign up for a government debt forgiveness program that requires her to work for a government agency or nonprofit for 10 years and have her debt forgiven. Of course, these programs have their pros and cons and many intricate details. And while they may not be the best option for everyone, I encourage you to research these and see if they might be useful to you. If you are going to work for the government or social sector, why not explore it? You never know. I am also confident, or maybe just hopeful, that the Department of Education will continue to innovate in their efforts to help people pay off their educational loans.

6) Commitment is essential in paying off debts. Make sure you commit to repaying your debts; otherwise, you will catch yourself in a vicious cycle of playing catch up with your bills.

When I was searching for colleges, I wished many times that I had the opportunity to just take out loans to pay for college. However, this was not an option due to my immigration status at the time, so I had to get creative. In retrospect, I feel enormously fortunate that I was able to complete my degrees without debt, but I also know how incredibly uncomfortable and trying this process was.

In an ideal world--the world I advise you to explore--you would find ways to pay at least 90% of your schooling without taking loans out and then use loans only when necessary. Student loans can be a source of support given the context of your situation, but they are certainly not the only route, as I have discussed in the chapter on paying for your education. Many people, not realizing that loans need to be paid back with interest or that there are alternatives, jump at them and often take a lot more than they need.

Don't be one of those people.

It is easy to take a loan early on, but when you start paying it off, you will regret that you weren't more thoughtful about how much you should have taken out. This will also affect your feelings about your educational experience.

26. CAR LOANS

> *Always borrow money from a pessimist; he*
> *doesn't expect to be paid back.*
> UNKNOWN

I bought my first (and only) car right after college.

A few days after graduation, I landed a full-time job and was ecstatic to get a car, a brand new car, of my own. At that time, I lived in Green Bay, Wisconsin so I genuinely needed a car. I also like driving and spent years before that time driving other people's cars. Having a car, however, was also a status symbol for me; I had accomplished something (e.g. finished college) and with a car of my own I had a degree of freedom. I also did not want to deal with it breaking down hence a desire for a brand new one.

In many ways, this was an emotional rather than a practical experience. A car of my own would offer me the freedom to travel wherever I wanted, and would be another step toward fulfilling the "American Dream." Some people urged me to get a used car, a beater, or even not get a car at all, at least for a while, and continue to carpool instead. I was not having any of that and after about a month of research, I purchased a brand new Subaru Impreza with a sunroof and an iPad plug in.

I was so excited!

I told everyone about my "Suby."

I was also $24,000 in debt at a 2.8% interest rate.

Looking back, I have no regrets because, at an emotional level, this is what I needed at the time. However, from a practical standpoint, I think I could have accomplished the same had I purchased a used car. I ended up selling Suby one day before I moved to Chicago for graduate school. Even though I had driven over 15,000 miles annually and had been in a fender bender, I had kept the car in a good shape and was able to find a great couple who took the car off of my hands at a fair price. And, I suffered the loss of "only" $1,000. That is to say, I had to pay an extra thousand dollars (on top of their payment for the car) in order to fully repay my car loan and release the car lien to the new owners. I was fortunate, because it is said that the moment you drive the new car off of a lot it loses value by 20%. In my case, this would have been $4,800. Thankfully, my loss was only $1,000 after two years of ownership.

Most people will encourage you to get a beater car and so on. I won't encourage you to do that-because having a beater can, and usually does, come with additional expenses and responsibility--however, I would advise you to follow these tips when considering car ownership and purchase:

1) To get a car or not? Do you really need a car? When I was in Green Bay, I knew I realistically needed a car. Due to the nature of my work at that time and fairly unpredictable public transportation, climate, and the spread-out city, it would have been very hard to get around without a car. However, when I moved to Chicago, because the opposite was true (except for the climate), I knew I did not need a car. Some people still hold on to it, however, out of convenience or for emotional reasons. But to me, this was a matter of pure economics and math. Upon my move to Chicago, my rent went up by 120%. Adding monthly car payments, car insurance, and parking--the latter of which would have gone up by 1,000%--was simply not feasible. Don't get me wrong, I loved my Suby. But after creating two rubrics, "pro car" and "con car," and accounting for the money I would likely spend using public transport, taxis, and a car-sharing service called Zip Car, giving up my car was a huge saving. In terms of real numbers, between my car payments, insurance, and very basic parking, I would have spent at least $750/month whereas the other route cost me, at most, $150/month. If you are in a similar position, do the math; your decision will be very clear.

2) Do your research. Purchasing a car is a process and if you decide to get a car, take your time to research it. I almost bought a gray Subaru, on impulse, the first time I saw it -- but I am glad I waited until the time was right and I could get the "perfect one." Before getting Suby, however, I spent a lot of time understanding my needs and financial ability. I knew that I could not pay more than $350/month in car payments. I also knew that after ending up in a couple of car accidents due to poor breaks afforded by a borrowed beater I drove before, I wanted an all-wheel drive; I wanted an awesome music system, and possibly a sun roof. I also wanted a good quality car. At first, I was in love with both Rav4 and Santa Fe. However, I couldn't afford either. Subaru prevailed. Then, I researched car dealers and asked for referrals. I talked to people about car brands, researched online, and asked a lot of questions about interest rates and loan sources. I also negotiated.

3) New Car or Used Car. Today, I would advise you to consider a used car, but this depends on your view of cars and your needs. A car can be a necessity and, therefore, our monthly expenses associated with meeting this necessity are a natural part of life. That said, we should do our best to have a car that we can afford, a car that meets our needs, not our wants, and a car that essentially does the job we need it to do. You should not mistake this as an argument for getting the cheapest car out there. If you drive a lot, I would strongly encourage you to get a comfortable and reliable car. If you foresee yourself transporting a lot of stuff, get a car that can fit it all. If you do not see yourself rolling up your sleeves to fix the car if it breaks down on the road, I would consider a new car. If you are driving a lot, then I would consider a car that gets good gas mileage. If you hope to use the car until it dies, then buying a new vehicle or used vehicle within a few model years makes sense because you can make sure to maintain it so it lasts longer, and so on.

In other words, understanding your needs and abilities is essential. What are you "hiring" your car to do for you and what are you willing to do to maintain its health? Some people would rather fix their own car as opposed to paying more for a new car and warranty. It is not always about the price tag. Although some people will tell you otherwise, in my opinion, having a car is not only about getting a job done, it is also about quality of life. While you certainly do not need a Porsche to meet your needs, it is OK to get creative and get a car that you can both afford and that is comfortable. This is especially true if you will be driving daily and for longer periods of time (e.g. if your commute to work is longer, etc.)

A good start to understanding your needs is by honestly answering these questions:

a) Do I need a car?

b) Why do I need / want a car?

c) Is public transportation an option at all?

d) Is it cheaper, more expensive, or equally as expensive to have a car?

e) What are top three "must haves" in my new car?

f) How much can I really afford?
How much am I willing to spend?

g) Is it better to get a lease, used car, or new car?

h) Can I carpool or share car with someone?

i) How much will I / can I spend in gas?
What about maintenance?

j) Where can I get a car without or really low interest rates?

4) Get a car without interest rates. I keep seeing all these commercials that talk about 0% interest rates. Explore those. Banks and dealers will tell you they are giving you the best deal...trust, but verify. Their interest is to sell you a loan, not manage your finances. You can't blame them.. Do your job by shopping around and try to get the lowest possible rate. Sometimes, holding off a few weeks or months on a purchase can change the rate you receive.

5) All things being equal, buy a cheaper car. I am all for comfort and getting a car that meets your reasonable needs. However, do your best to find the cheapest car. Even $500 cheaper will make a difference in the long run. This brings me to...

6) Negotiate. People make much of negotiation, but basic negotiating skills are pretty simple: do not put yourself in a position where you are desperate and have to agree to anything. Go shopping when you are level-headed and go in with a clear understanding of the maximum monthly payment you could manage (e.g. for me, it was $350/month). Don't easily trust when they talk about "deals" and "specials;" instead make an offer that is tangibly below what you can afford. For example, I walked in to a dealership claiming that I wouldn't pay more than $290/month; they wanted me to pay $375. We met at $324 and some change. This was a win because it was still $26 cheaper than my high limit. Be willing to walk away, too, although know that this won't be so hard to do if you have done a good job researching all your options. And, more than anything, do not go in buying big items on impulse. You are likely to get a bad deal.

7) Pay off your loan as soon as you can. I have been repeating this all throughout this chapter: when you owe money with interest, pay it off as soon as possible. The longer you finance your car, the more money will you end up paying. So, pay your loan as soon as you can. This is especially true if you buy a new car and/or carry high interest.

8) Take care of your car. Regardless of the type of car you buy, take care of it. Proper maintenance can affect your car's health in a positive way and have positive consequences on your wallet, too. This is one of the lessons I learned from my Dad, who used to have a business selling spare parts for cars and trucks, and his lessons rang true when I tried to sell my car: it was in a great condition. Get your oil changed and check the other liquids in the car; make sure to pay attention to your breaks, to wash your car, and avoid getting it scratched up or hit on sidewalks or in parking ramps. Look at it as your baby. You can also give it a name; this forms an emotional connection and helps in caring more carefully for it.

27. CREDIT SCORE

Your reputation is like credit score.
Everything you do can affect it.
MICHELLE PARSONS

In today's world, it is important to establish and build credit in order to obtain low financing rates on consumer purchases (such as a house or car), increase candidacy as a job applicant or when applying for a rental unit, maintain low insurance premiums, and even apply for utility services.

We live in a society where financial capability is closely tied to our credit history, credit reporting, and credit scoring. Greater financial capability requires that we have good credit. And having good credit means that we have demonstrated over time and in more than one way that we pay off our debts on time, are thoughtful about how we use credit extended to us, and consistently have our financial house in order. There are agencies that monitor our debt management --credit cards, auto loans, mortgage, student loans, etc.--and report what they see via a "credit report," which is a detailed report of our financial reliability.

There are three main credit reporting agencies in the U.S.: Experian, Equifax, and TransUnion. You can request one credit report annually from each of these agencies for free at annualcreditreport.com. By reviewing your credit report, you can see all of the lines of credit you currently have open (as well as lines you have had in the past), you can check to see if all of your creditors are accurately reporting your repayment, and check for errors. I once heard a story about a man who had someone else's delinquent medical bill show up on his credit report. Thankfully, he was able to contact the credit reporting agencies and notify them of the error. Had he not reviewed his report, his credit would have been negatively affected by the outstanding medical bill and could have hampered his ability to access credit.

The credit reporting agencies also calculate a credit score, which banks and lending agencies will use to help them determine how much credit they will extend to you and at what interest rate. A credit score takes the following factors into account:

• *Payment History (35%)* – this includes payment information on rent, credit cards, retail accounts, installment loans, and finance company accounts including details on late or missed payments as well as accounts which show no late payments.

• *Amounts Owed (30%)* – Credit utilization considers the amount owed in comparison with the amount of credit available. This category analyzes the balance owed on all accounts, whether there is a balance on certain types of accounts, the remaining balance on installment loan accounts compared to the original balance, and the percentage of credit being used out of total available credit.

• *Length of Credit History (15%)* – Generally, a longer credit history will cause a credit score to increase. Credit scoring agencies consider the age of the oldest account, the age of the newest account, and the average age of the accounts as well as the length of time since a certain account has been used.

• *New Credit (10%)* – Research shows that opening several credit accounts in a short period of time represents a greater credit risk, especially among those with a short credit history. This category examines the number of new accounts a person has, the number of recent requests they have made for credit, the length of time since credit report inquiries were made by lenders, and whether they have good recent credit history, following past payment problems. If a person is shopping for credit and has multiple credit inquiries on their report within a 30 day period, they will be included as one inquiry.

• *Types of Credit in Use (10%)* – This part of a credit score analyzes the types of credit a consumer has experience with including both revolving and installment credit. It also examines the number of credit lines a consumer carries within each type of credit.

Your credit report can be summarized by a credit score. There are several agencies that use algorithms to calculate our scores, but you may have heard of the most famous one: FICO score. These scores help put us in various categories so that when we apply for a loan, a credit card, or similar, the financial institutions can review our credit score and history and decide if they should extend us that loan (or a credit line) and under what terms they should extend it (i.e. interest rates and loan length). The better our score and credit history, the easier it is for us to access credit and access credit with more favorable loan terms.

These tips have helped me in managing my own credit, and I hope they will help you too:

1) Know your credit. Federal law entitles you to access your credit report, for free, once a year. Also, many credit card companies have begun offering credit score on your statements as a way to help you remain informed about your credit. Additionally, there are several agencies that offer credit monitoring service for a monthly fee. These are not necessary. What you can do is sign up for a free trial or one month, understand what is going on with your credit, and cancel your subscription. Or just go to www.annualcreditreport.com and get your report and rely on other sources for your score. This is important for two reasons: (a) there may be mistakes on your report that affect your credit and borrowing ability. If you identify them, you can call the reporting agency and they can have it fixed; (b) by knowing your credit score and report, you will know what you might qualify for and you can work to improve it if you plan a purchase or similar.

2) *Take charge of your credit.* Regardless of past experiences, even bankruptcy, rebuilding your credit is possible. There are several simple rules on how you can do this:

(a) Pay all your bills on time;

(b) Do not allow your bill to go into collection;

(c) Monitor your credit report for mistakes;

(d) Do not carry credit card balance;

(e) If you have to, carry a balance that's less than 30% of your credit line;

(f) Spread your balance over several credit cards instead of maxing one of them

(g) Do not close your credit cards even if you don't use them;

(h) Do not apply for a new credit card or loan all the time; if you do, keep them close to each other;

(i) Check your score before you apply for a loan, so that you can avoid getting rejected;

(j) It is not only credit cards, student loans, and mortgages that are included on your report; watch for medical bills, phone bills, and the like--if you fail to pay any of them and they are sent into collections, this event may show up on your credit report and negatively affect your credit history and

credit score. So, again: pay your bills on time.

3) Manage your credit cards in order to better your credit score. Having a credit card is a good thing because it builds your credit history, demonstrates your potential trustworthiness in repaying any future loans, and it gives you a line of credit that can come in handy for a number of reasons. However, it is essential to manage your credit cards in a way that is beneficial to you. For example, maxing any one of your cards or all of them will affect your credit score negatively. So, as a rule, try to keep your balance to less than 30% of your overall credit limit. If you have to use more, open additional cards but then freeze them (literally, so that you can't access them easily); this will expand your credit line thus changing the usage / available credit ratio. Do not close any of the cards. Keep them active by making a couple of annual purchases and pay them off right away. This activity on the card will keep your card issuer from closing it and it will allow you to maintain the same credit line. Every time you apply for a card, the financial institution makes a "hard inquiry" that affects your credit score. That is to say, your score goes down. So, if you are applying for credit cards or shopping for a loan, do so within 30 days, because these hard inquiries will have only one hard hit on your credit report. However, do not open too many credit cards at once, because that may negatively affect your score (you may be viewed as desperate).

That is above 50% of your credit limit--ideally, you will keep it below 15% of your credit line.

The best way to build your credit is to have a credit card, use it every month, but always pay off your balance. Some people are under the impression that carrying a balance is what builds your credit. This is not true! Having a balance is what can negatively affect your credit, especially if you do not pay on time.

3) Credit paradox. There are a couple of other rules surrounding credit, some of them paradoxical: For example, the higher your credit line, the higher your score but only if you use a small portion of your credit line. The older your credit history, the better your score but only if there are no negative marks of late bills or collections or bankruptcy on your report. The higher your "revolving credit line" (a term for credit provided through credit cards) the better, but if you open too many cards in a short period of time, your credit may suffer. Your student loans, car loans, and mortgage are good for your credit, but only if you pay them on time, every single time. It is a good idea for your parents or other adults to help you open a credit card; however, adding you to their credit card will not build your credit history (although this was the case in the past).

This is just the basic list of rules and tips on credit management. This is by no means an all-inclusive list, however, but I believe it contains the basics that can help you manage your own credit effectively. I have been at both sides of the spectrum, where my credit was nearly 800 and fell down to low 600 when I maxed my credit cards. Life happens and your credit will be affected accordingly. However, if you take a few hours a year to review your credit and are prudent with your financial management, you can do your part in maintaining a good credit, fixing a damaged credit, and bettering your current credit thus affording yourself opportunities for loans, lower rates, and a degree of financial freedom.

28. INVESTING IN
   YOUR FUTURE

> *Retirement is not in my vocabulary. They aren't
> going to get rid of me that way.*
> BETTY WHITE

In working with iOme Challenge on raising awareness about financial security in retirement, , I have heard people use the old adage "a penny saved is a penny earned" when encouraging people to save for their future. This saying is cliché indeed, but has become so because it is true.

Most of us know that saving money is a good thing. It is also necessary. And by reading this book, you also know about the power of compound interest and what it can do for you in the long run. At the same time, however, I am sure you also realize how difficult it is to save money.

Between your housing expenses, food, clothing, phone, internet, car, entertainment, student loans, and credit card debt, you are stretched thin. In fact, you are probably likely to have nothing left to save or are getting yourself into debt regularly, are borrowing money, or have someone bail you out. According to a recent study by iOme Challenge, 23% of us born between 1982 and 2000 have our parents or someone else helping us pay our monthly bills.

Or perhaps you think that saving $15 would not make a difference. Or that you will save some day, but can't do it just yet. Or, even worse, that you will become a millionaire so you won't need to save.

I agree with all these things.

Here's the problem: unless we save today, we are going to have a major problem in the future. I am not kidding you. I can overwhelm you with all the statistics that show how critical it is that we save. For example, an average 55 year old in the United States has less than $10,000 in retirement savings today. Many older people are going back into the workforce in order to pay their bills and have more discretionary income. One of the main reasons why a lot of people are still able to retire at 65 or 67 years of age is because Social Security is fully solvent and can support their retirement lifestyle, in part because there are so many of us young people who keep paying into it. Another big reason is because we are seeing the greatest transfer of wealth in the American history right now, too, allowing the Boomers to retire by benefiting from the savings of their parents. But what happens if our parents spend all that money? There wouldn't be much savings left for us.

Another major concern about not saving and investing (early) in our future stems from the fact that together, as a society, we will have a major economic problem that will affect our collective well being and the strength of the country. Because it is several decades off, it does not seem problematic. However, the only way to solve the problem before it happens—and transform the problem into an opportunity—is to think early and think ahead. This is what leadership is about.

Now, I am not trying to scare you, because I believe we will ultimately be fine; however, I am trying to encourage you to take control of your future in following ways:

Saving and Investing for Retirement
Does your employer have a retirement plan? Ask the

director of HR and if they do, contribute 6%. It seems a lot, but you will get used to living without it. Just go ahead and sign up. Don't ask too many questions or ponder if you should, just do it. Often, employers match your contributions up to 3% or 6% of salary, and you want to invest at least up to their matching level. This will be done automatically, your paycheck will be slightly smaller, but you won't notice it after two months. Seriously. Do it.

No one wants to think about getting old, wrinkly, and needing help. However, this future is inevitable, and the easiest way to make sure we have one while not thinking much about it is to save for it, today. The sooner we do it, the better, because of ... compound interest, of course. For example, if you are 27 years old today making $50,000/year, and you save $4,500 annually at the average rate of 9% until you are 67, you will end up with $1,520,471.00. That's a nice chunk of money. I am not a financial advisor so I would urge you to speak to one who can explain this in more detail, specifically as it relates to you and your individual goals and dreams, and also your income.

At the very least, however. Google "retirement calculator" and use those to play around with numbers and see what your retirement might look like financially. Another option is to use predictions on the Social Security Administration website as a way to calculate your social security benefits. In either case, figure out what IRA (Individual Retirement Account) stands for, what Roth-IRA is, what MyRA is, what 401k is, and how each of these can best work for you.

Another interesting factoid is that the person who saves between the ages of 25 and 35 will have more money saved up when they turn 65 than the person who saved at the same rate from ages 35 to 65. Of course, it is *never* too late start saving for your retirement.

The elephant in the room: some of us may never want to retire. The retirement age of 65 was artificially set when Social Security was established and it was modeled on Otto Von

Bismarck's establishment of a retirement system in the Imperial Germany. However, since the average life expectancy was 61 years of age at the time of formation of Social Security, it precluded many people from reaping the benefits in retirement. Today, with a significantly higher life expectancy, there are more people retiring later or going back into the workforce, or spending a lot of time volunteering, because that keeps them engaged and away from boredom.

All this leads to a question: *why should we save for retirement if we are going to re-imagine it and perhaps never retire in the traditional sense?*

The answer is: *freedom.*

Whatever you want your later years to be like is entirely up to you. However, having money in the bank will give you the freedom of choice.

Do you want to spend years in Florida, on the beach? Do you prefer to work until you drop dead? Do you hope to travel the world or leave a lot of money to your kids or support your favorite charities?

All of these are viable options, but by being adequately prepared, you will be able to make a choice that works best for you as opposed to being forced into a particular choice by your circumstances. And, the good news is: you do not have to be Warren Buffet or have his investment-savvy to save and invest some money. All you need is a decision to do so and a little bit of effort to put everything in place (e.g. speaking to your HR department, getting a financial advisor or coach, and so on). Investing is only complicated if you make it so.

Emergency Savings

This one is pretty straightforward. Life happens and for whatever reason we may find ourselves without an income for a period of time. In order to address those times of hardship, you should have some money in the bank to carry you over. Credit cards can do some of this, but, for example, you cannot pay your rent with a credit card. Thus, be intentional and deliberate in employing some of the savings strategies that listed below in order to accumulate a decent amount of emergency savings. Some people suggest that you should save up to six-months worth of living expenses. I say, do that, but then take three months from it and invest into a mutual fund or some other type of investment vehicle that would make your money work for you, but can still be accessed without penalties. The idea behind my logic is that even if you get laid off, hopefully you won't need more three months to get back on your feet. And if you do, then you can use those first three months to access some of your mutual fund investments. In either case, by employing this approach, you will increase your chances of having your money work for you.

Note: I know you think that your "high yield savings account" is saving you a lot of money, because it sounds like it would. However, savings accounts don't generally save that much as compared to investment accounts. Sure, they don't bear high risk, but even the best savings accounts might give you, at most, 2% annual savings rate. An investment average over the last 40 years in the United States has been about 10%. Do the math! Of course, the problem with investment accounts is that you don't want to have to pull the money out on a whim, and you may also lose it, which is why having some cash in the bank makes sense for easy access.

How to Save?

Late M. Scott Peck, famous psychiatrist and best-selling author of *The Road Less Traveled*, asked his patients a question: *how do you eat your cake? Do you go right away for the icing, do you eat the cake part first, or do you have a measured approach?*

When he observed one of his clients going right for the icing, he understood that she had a challenge with delaying gratification. Saving, especially when it comes to saving for retirement, has everything to do with habits and with delaying gratification. Why would I wait 30 or 40 years to enjoy my life?

YOLO: You Live Only Once, so spend it all now, right?

When you are 20, this totally makes sense, because you tell

yourself that you can just save later, right? However, if you look at the facts, you know that saving makes a lot more sense in the long run, especially when you start early. The momentary satisfaction is fleeting; stability in the long-term is a lot more rewarding and it last much longer.

During one of the iOme Challenge contests, a winning team wrote about financial neuroscience in relation to saving vs. our emotional impulses. To get a lot better explanation of their Elephant and Rider logic, visit www.iomechallenge.org to read the paper. Here, however, I will illustrate this analogy in simplified terms: the elephant represents your emotional impulses and the rider is you will. When it comes to saving, you need to listen to the rider. You need to employ the power of your will and not let the big elephant carry you away.

There's a reason why they illustrated our emotions with an elephant: because they are enormous and rule our lives. And they are quick. However, it is the rider who guides the elephant and needs to remain in control.

This logic equates to our conversation about values guiding our emotions which then guide our actions from the earlier chapter. If your value is to save—if you choose saving as your value—then this value, through the power of your will, will guide your emotions, which will then guide your actions. This logic works for other things beyond saving, too. However, most of us pay lip service to saving without really believing wholeheartedly in its relevance, importance, or necessity. Therefore, saving never really becomes our value. To makes things worse: saving is hard, especially when the gratification part does not happen until a lot later or, as in the case of emergency savings, maybe (and hopefully) never. It also requires a habit.

Here, I am asking you to do something that is totally counterintuitive, something that is very hard, especially as the money is tight for most of us, and something that you may potentially never benefit from. Yes, that is exactly what I am asking you because, just like with eating fruits and vegetables and learning to love it, you may not see the benefit, but you also won't see what happens if you ate fast food instead. In the case of not eating fast food, you will avoid obesity and health problems that are certain to come with it. In the case of saving, you will avoid poverty and financial headaches.

So, how do we save?

Make it easy.

Automate your savings by signing up for a retirement plan through your employer or by consulting a financial advisor, or even by going online and enrolling into an IRA plan with a financial institution. Something. Anything. Then, set up automatic withdrawals from your bank account into your savings account, so that you don't have to even think about it.

Intentionally delay gratification by rewarding yourself. In other words, train yourself to not spend money on impulse by planning a particular purchase, anticipating it, and after you reach a particular savings goal, rewarding yourself with it. For example, if your goal was to save $500 at the end of the month, and you reached the goal, go ahead and treat yourself to something that is perhaps 10% of that saving. In other words, you are delaying gratification in exchange for something. I use this logic when working out: I love to drink protein shakes that come after a workout. So, if I am in the mood for one, I first have to work out to get it!

Use a budget. I know, sounds scary, but we discussed it earlier. It is a necessary evil. Even if you made millions of dollars, you'd still need it. So, if you want financial success, stop avoiding it and use the power of your will to get into budgeting. It is not that difficult and you will get used to it, I promise.

Another way to get into a habit of saving is by putting a little money here and there on the side, in a separate savings account that is hard to access. I know how hard it can be to save—believe me, I do—but you can use little games to save. For example, this year, I have been doing the 52-week challenge, where I put the amount of money in an envelope that corresponds to a particular week of the year. For example, on January 1, I put $1 away. On the 30th week, I put $30 away. By the end of the year, I am supposed to have $1,378 saved up! One thing I noticed about this exercise is that it gets tough when I get into the latter weeks, so next year, I plan on doing it in reverse: on Jan 1, I will put $52 away. On the last week of the year, I will put $1 away. This reverse approach will be a bit easier, I think. because I will be excited and find a way to start off strong in January and the excitement will carry on throughout the year, because the amount I will be putting away will continuously decrease. You can also commit to save all your change or even save on one latte a week, for example. All of these little acts of saving will accumulate and soon enough you might have enough in the bank to pay your rent for a month or two.

Some people would tell you that you shouldn't play these tricks…these games, but just save 20% of your income by putting it aside through a retirement account and also savings account. This sounds great. But what if you can't afford to do that…or, which is more often the case, if you do not have a habit of doing so? By engaging in fun savings activities, especially if you do it with your friends, you have a better chance of developing a habit of saving on a regular basis—and even just thinking about it.

I am a believer that the best way to save money is to make more money. This, however, is not an option for most of us. Therefore, the second best option is to learn to prioritize, delay gratification, and make savings easy. You can even make goals, share them with your significant other or close friends, or even on social media if you want, and work for that goal.

Saving doesn't have to be so scary.

You can even teach yourself delayed gratification by actually paying attention to how you eat your cake or your meals: do you leave the best for the last?

AFTERWORD:
WHAT'S YOUR GPA?

Writing this guide has been a journey of a thousand miles, condensed into a few short weeks. It was much harder than I expected it to be. It was also a lot more rewarding than I thought it would be. As I went searching for stories in the darkest corners of my memory, in the effort to bring about lessons that may be helpful to you, I found myself deeply humbled and grateful for the experience of introspection; one that I could not have had without this project.

This guide went through many identities, many revisions, and much struggle, in order to reach its present look. When I began writing it, I hesitated, because I was slightly unsure of the value it would bring or the quality of lessons it would impart. But, because I engaged in this process, I was able to witness how I developed over the last ten years.

In retrospect, it all makes sense.

My journey all the way from the European Black Mountain through Wisconsin's dairy land and then to the Second City, has been tough. But it has also been incredibly rewarding. And I am grateful for every bit of it. It has taught me a lot. It has transformed me. And, which is more, it has afforded me a better life and a full measure of freedom, happiness, and love.

That same thing which I desired as a 15-year old standing on the shores of the Adriatic.

I guess, dreams do come true.

~

I believe that you, too, should pursue your own dreams and a full measure of happiness, unapologetically. And to assist with that, I wanted to end this guide with my formula for happiness:

Goodness + Purpose + Action = Happiness

I can -- and plan to -- write an entire book on our fundamental goodness, which is a main driver behind our happiness, and you can read more about my musings on this topic on my blog iamgoodproject.com.

In the meantime, however, to understand the formula, I will share this: our origin is goodness and our purpose is growth, but our journey is without a destination. The real question is not where we are headed, but how do we make our journey count? I believe that the answer lies in looking at life through the lens of goodness. That is to say, when we accept and live out our individual goodness and find ways to do so every day, with every interaction, in every situation, and under all conditions, we see our lives transformed, joy and peace emerge, and happiness prevails.

It is impossible to be fully happy and content unless we believe, at some level, that we are fundamentally good. If we do not believe in our own fundamental goodness, how can we believe that we are worthy of happiness?

Once we have goodness in place, we discover our purpose. As we drew from the chapter on this topic, discovering our purpose is a pressing matter. It is essential to know why we are here.

Then, we act. Nothing happens without action.

Happiness, just like love, is a verb.

When we begin with goodness, it is easy to be honest with ourselves about our purpose; once we are clear on our purpose and fueled with our inner goodness, it is only natural that we will want to act vigorously.

Goodness is our foundation, purpose is our direction, and action is our path to happiness.

Sometimes, the reverse works too. Even if we are unsure about your purpose or goodness -- it is okay and important to admit this so that you can transform it -- taking action and doing the things that make sense to you and feel right will lead to greater clarity. Every step, every action, every movement creates motion, and this motion creates change. It leads us somewhere new -- and often right to our purpose and to our goodness.

It is through this action and alignment that happiness ensues.

So, what is *your* GPA?

ACKNOWLEDGMENTS

This project would not have come to life without the help of many people. I am especially grateful to Allison, B, Vasilije, Bojan, and Chris for reading, editing, and offering feedback; and to unsurpassed Tami Jo for the cover design, and exceptionally talented Jared for the headshot.

Mom and Dad, thank you for your unyielding support and love. Silvija and Emil, thank you for stopping along the way to offer a helping hand to your little brother; Jason and Nicole, thank you for never protesting. Alex, Ryan, Mia, and Michael (and Marv) -- I love you.

Mis'a and Djuro, thank you for believing in me since I was a little boy. And Vera, thank you for teaching me the love of reading and writing, and for encouraging me to dream big; your wisdom has defined my journey.

Cindy and Tom, thank you for welcoming me to America, along with Grandma and Grandpa Badger and your family.

My St. Norbert community, thank you for accepting me as one of your own and for nurturing and challenging me as I prepared for every good work. It is because of you that my story is possible.

My iOme family, our supporters, participants, and the board -- thank you for believing in the cause and working to give our generation a better future.

Dave and Sue, thank you for believing in this budding

entrepreneur.

To all of you who have given me the opportunity to work with you in owning your own life; I am proud and privileged to have been a part of your journey. You *are* good!

My inner circle: *obviously*, Grom, my three-year old Akita whose fearlessness, unconditional love, and loyalty remind me of my values daily. Sabrina and D, thank you for the consistent encouragements. Jody, thank you for your unmatched enthusiasm and help. Gratzia, thank you your unwavering faith and for being like my second Mom. Vasilije, our paths have been intertwined from the beginning ... the best is to yet come. Steve, thank you for your loyalty. Kevin, with you, friendship knows no bounds. Trevor, thank you for the stable presence and for opening doors every step of the way. Allison, my buddy, you are a gem and I am grateful for you. B, thank you for believing in me, and for encouraging me to own it and to dare greatly from the very beginning. And, Chris, you are my shining star. Thank you for keeping me grounded and for inspiring the better angels of my nature.

I love you all.

Lastly, I thank my Creator and the Universe for all the goodness, all the blessings, and every experience that has brought me to where I am today.

ABOUT THE AUTHOR

Adi Redzic is a social entrepreneur, speaker, and coach. He is also the Executive Director of iOme Challenge, an award-winning effort to raise awareness about the long-term financial security of the Generation Y.

He lives in Chicago, IL.

You can follow him on Twitter @thinkchange or visit his blog at iamgoodproject.com

Made in the USA
Charleston, SC
29 September 2014